SECOND**FACE**

BY: AKOMA

1

The Second Face

A book about romance scam on the Internet

by AKOMA NTOSO

First edition published in July 2020

Contact the authors: mn804581@gmail.com

Abstract:

Romance scam is growing all over the world. Attractive women or men send friend requests on *Instagram, Facebook, Twitter* and other dating sites. Once *the client* (the victim) has approved this request, he or she is quickly transferred to another chat platform like *Hangouts, WhatsApp* or *Telegram*. The scamming process has started. In the worst case the victim will never find out that the attractive person on the pictures or on the video calls has *a second face*, mostly a black one or that the attractive woman in reality is a man. *Fake lover's oaths* and so-called *formats* lead the victim into a one-way street from where a return to normal live becomes nearly impossible because the scammers will not give up before they get what they want: *money*.

We (AKOMA NTOSO – The linked hearts) decided to write this book to show what *romance scam* is, how it works, who *the victims* are, who *the scammers* are and *the different possibilities of scam* and *the causes behind* this phenomenon and an exciting insight into the real world of scammer groups like the *Yahoo Boys* in Nigeria or the *Illuminati* in Ghana.

This book is intended to educate people all over the world regarding the process of romance scam and thus to act preventively against love scams on the

Internet by providing first-hand background knowledge.

May this world become a better one, one day!

List of contents

.

1. The Phenomenon Romance Scam – how Scammers get in Contact with their Victims

The phenomenon of *romance scam* on the Internet is more topical than ever before. Large sums of money flow annually from all over the world to Africa, but also to other countries like India, China or Russia etc. Scammer strongholds on the African continent are Ghana and Nigeria, where many young people do not find adequate work despite good education and see how others simply obtain money from their homes via mobile phones, tablets or laptops and apparently earn good money in this way.

How does that work? It's simple. After creating a Facebook, Instagram, Twitter or similar account on a paid dating site with a stolen identity and fake pictures, a friend request is sent or a message is written:

> Hello pretty lady you've got the most prettiest smile I have ever seen are you from heaven?

> Hello there!Wow 😊 your eyes •• are so beautiful and expressive .Your hair is so much nice 👍 .You must have spent a so much time to make such a beautiful hair.

After a few word exchanges on the Internet platform, the beloved *king* or *queen* is quickly *dragged away* to either Hangouts, WhatsApp or

Telegram, ostensibly because the new acquaintance cannot always be on Instagram or Facebook etc., but in reality to be undisturbed with his/her victim and because the online account can be deleted at any time. Deleted? Yes, because the new heart friend chats with up to 20 people at the same time and is often reported as fake account and usually deleted afterwards. He or she has many accounts on different platforms with different identities. Behind the fake profiles there are mostly black people, Indians, Malaysian, Chinese or Russian people. Scammers are generally very superstitious and believe that on some profiles there is *luck* on it to bring them the money.

> For me WhatsApp is nice, but you can write where you like.
>
> Nov. 11, 8.55 Nachm

> I'm going to have dinner now

OK

> Take good care of yourself
> 🖤

The pictures of an account can change monthly as shown below. It is the same account monitored over months. The first fake account shows a stolen and abused picture of the model and actor Brian Haugen, the real identity of the other persons is unknown and therefore not shown in a distinct way to protect their privacy.

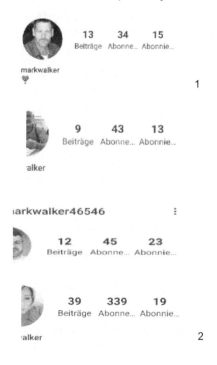

1

2

Once the scammer has his victim on a chat platform like WhatsApp, he usually proceeds quickly. An intensive online relationship with expressions of love and marriage promises is established. He

---

[1] https://www.brianhaugen.net/
[2] Fake pictures on Instagram

usually uses a *format* he goes by. This format is like a written instruction, for example, if he wants to get money for his sick child later. He builds up and manipulates his victim step by step in the direction he wants to have it, by isolating and brainwashing the client. The victim becomes dependent on the scammer and his *love* and the scam can be executed easily because the victim doesn't want to lose the *beloved person.*

> I don't want to appreciate
> what I have after I have
> lost it, so I am keeping you
> forever. You are my best
> and none else fit.

Some scams are done within some weeks, others can take years, where no money is asked. The scammer manipulates the chat platform and does not appear online, though he is always online there. The chat platform is *cracked* and so no one sees him online. The fraud will do everything to convince the victim of his love. Even pictures are manipulated with the name and the actual date and sent to the client to convince him or her that the scammer is a *real person.* If the fake is about ill people in the hospital, the fake picture is edited with the face of an ill person. There are many people working behind the scam. Some do design of pictures, fake identity cards or fake real estate documents, others just assist in chatting, others do fake phone calls, others *acquire new clients* to be transported to WhatsApp or Hangouts etc. If the scammer for example is a man pretending to a client that he is a *woman*, he will have females there, who do the fake phone call for him. For that he has to pay these women.

Once a scammer did not remember that he was speaking to a woman and confused her with a man. So, the woman knew, that he was also speaking to a man at the same time.

As soon as the scammer is sure that his *client* has fallen in love, he quickly *gets into financial trouble*. Imagination is required: The child is seriously ill and needs an operation, but unfortunately, he cannot access his bank account at the moment or he has been arrested by the police and has to pay a bail or the mobile phone suddenly doesn't work anymore etc. etc.

The following examples show

1) a military scammer who wants money for the birthday trip of his son

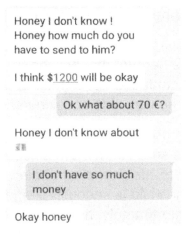

Honey I don't know !
Honey how much do you
have to send to him?

I think $1200 will be okay

Ok what about 70 €?

Honey I don't know about

I don't have so much
money

Okay honey

2) a military scammer who wants to send a box with a lot of money to the client

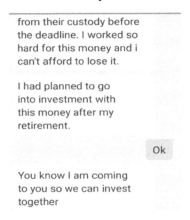

from their custody before
the deadline. I worked so
hard for this money and i
can't afford to lose it.

I had planned to go
into investment with
this money after my
retirement.

Ok

You know I am coming
to you so we can invest
together

3) a military scammer reproaching heartlessness and unkindness to the victim in order to make him or her feel guilty and responsible

What happens after the victim has paid? If the money has arrived at the scammer via, for example, Western Union Bank, PayPal, Chili, Cash App, Bitcoin, Gift card or cheque there are two possibilities: either the victim is sucked further until there is nothing left to get and then blocked or immediately blocked and deleted. Goodbye, *my love*!

Western Union Bank has restricted the money transfer to Nigeria and Ghana due to scams. If the scammer wants to pick up the money there, the police will ask him, from where and for what he received this money. Sometimes the money is sent back to the victim, sometimes the scammer pays the bank agent and the police officer and takes away the rest of the money. Scammer have so called *drops* in other countries, who take the money for them with different bank accounts, take their fee for it and pass the money on to the fraud. This is money laundry and a crime! There are people, who did that *out of love* for the scammer and were arrested.

Scammers exchange information online on groups or via chat programs like *Telegram*.

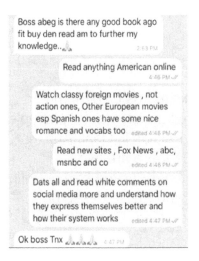

Boss abeg is there any good book ago fit buy den read am to further my knowledge... 2:53 PM

Read anything American online 4:46 PM

Watch classy foreign movies , not action ones, Other European movies esp Spanish ones have some nice romance and vocabs too edited 4:46 PM

Read new sites , Fox News , abc, msnbc and co edited 4:48 PM

Dats all and read white comments on social media more and understand how they express themselves better and how their system works edited 4:47 PM

Ok boss Tnx 4:47 PM

Let me break this down ..

🔨 90% of the clients online are just lonely , horny , very busy with work , got out of a divorce , so they need someone to just talk to , express emotions, entertain themselves ,

🔨 In summary 80% of em come online with no high hopes nor optimism. Along the day if your chat goes beyond and they really devel[o] some deep feelings they might decide to giv[e] it a try .

🔨 10% Are so scared of dying lonely , others ve some social class of friends prying (they wanna impress em) , others can't find noone in their neighborhood, sum just want sometin[g] fresh/young and a new breeze ,
They come online with high hopes , ready to do anything cos they pretty naive , desperate but they feel like they gotta find love
" *They are hard to find though* "

🔨 *That was just a " prologue " , to answer your question, We all get deceived by pals , because they talk big , say sweet words , brag , give us time but it's all like a lottery til[l] a client pays he's nothing but just another gamble . The 10% might act stupid /weird an[d] still pay ,The other 90% can give you all the hope and fail you utterly .*

🔨 *So just keep playing the jackpot, one day you will hit three apples , also this is why you need to be exclusive , get a plan so Incase y[o] meet a 10% , you hit big and stop this game for good , it's stressful*

Yo bro. If you are chatting a man with the beautician format and he asks how much you make in a month how much is good to say?
3:38 PM

Tell him it depends how good business is , Mostly since it's not a continuous work , when pageants arises you make good money about 5-8k in a month but on a dull month just 3-5k
But you still do individuals works and earn some bit of cash too
3:43 PM ✓

15

Am I supposed to give him my own drops location when he asks where exactly I live? I haven't seen something like that in the group yet. Kindly enlighten me.   8:49 PM

Find an apartment for rent on Craigslist or Zillow and use that as your address but also use the formats in the group to prevent him from driving to you
🔒Never let him send you any gift by mail
🔒Dont also send him anything by mail aswell   8:32 PM

Stop asking fresh clients for gifts cards as confirmation   7:58 PM

Stop asking fresh clients for phones as confirmation   7:58 PM

Stop asking fresh clients for flights money as confirmation he will book it for ya   7:59 PM

Stop asking fresh clients for phones as confirmation he's gonna worry u with unnecessary video calls and weird pics taking   7:59 PM

16

He said he wanted to send flowers that is why he is asking for the address

11:32 PM

Tell him flowers are better handed to in person with a hug and it shows more affection and romance so he should wait for you to come there so he can give you a romantic treat !!!!!

11:46 PM ✓

Boss client Dey ask how long my aunt get Parkinson's , what make I tell am

8:49 PM

He's asking about Medicare now

9:10 PM

Five years and tell him she's not on Medicare but private insurance.

Her insurance gets her medications and we just get her a private nurse ourself who takes times and look after her good and it's been part of her recovery to mild symptoms .

She gets the best treatment at home and she's managing and recovering good on her medications .
So I just pay the nurse all time and you need money for her to continue doing that because you are short of money a bit so you can come to him

9:35 PM ✓

17

2. Who are the Victims?

"Something like that can never happen to me, only fools fall for it" - But is that really true? Who are the potential victims of romance scammers?

Lonely hearts: Lonely women and men in middle and older age, who have not yet given up hope for *the great love*, are the biggest target group of love scammers. An online account on Instagram or Facebook for example and a lot of new subscribers come in. Why is this age group so attractive for scammers? The answer to this question is simple. At this age *one has already created something*, that attracts scammers because they are only interested

18

in one thing: MONEY! Love and real feelings do not play a role *in this online relationship*. That's why it doesn't matter to a 20-year-old black man if he writes to a 60-year-old white woman, who could be his grandmother, pretending to love her.

Theoretically, EVERYONE can become a victim, because these scammers sometimes take a very professional approach and it's not always immediately apparent that the *man* or *woman* at the other end of the phone or computer is in fact a cheat, who is only after financial rip-offs.

If the scammer finds a woman who seems to be *a big fish* for him, he quickly removes what he still loved one moment before:

3. Who are the Scammers?

There are different scammers from different countries as mentioned above. This book wants to show the scam in Ghana and Nigeria, introducing also the scammer groups of *the Illuminati* and *the Yahoo Boys.*

Mostly the scammers are young African men (but also women), who earn their living with this form of scamming. A man can also *become* a woman online and vice versa.

They consider themselves *entrepreneurs* and are happy to show their newly acquired wealth publicly. In their home country they cooperate with politicians, banks and even with the police and are well connected with other frauds. Scammers are often married and have a family and children. They try to earn money with the scam in order to have an income.

Since they are in contact with many different women worldwide at the same time, they have no feelings for the individual and no compassion for *the client,* who is emotionally and financially devastated after the scam. Normally the scammer has forgotten the victim after a few days. He simply does not care. *„She/he has fallen in love with a fake picture, not with me. I don't care. I am not guilty. This is not a crime. The white people stole everything from our country in the past, we get it back now",* are typical excuses.

The frauds communicate with each other in their own language using certain code words. The victim of the scam is called *client, voltage* indicates the wealth of the client, *level* expresses the course of the scam, *bomb* is used for hacking an internet account, *Mugu* or *Maga* means *fool* and means the victims of the scam. [3]

Yes I am the only one that feed my family

Try to find a way because the world is changing actually and this kind of work will not work anymore

I no but there is not a way out

But do you still find magas who pay?

I don't have anyone n

No?

I don't have any maga now

But thank God for protection me and my family

First the scammers ask a lot of questions, then they choose a form of scam that seems to work on the potential victim. However, they are flexible and can

---

[3] Uzochukwu (2018), S. 15 - 19

change their plans at any time if the chosen *scam format* does not work. They are smart and they don't give up easily. Some scams can take years till money is asked. The different types of scam will be explained in a separate chapter.

Some examples what scammers write on Instagram and Facebook:

What truth?

Show me who you are

You see I am real

Yes I'm black.

But I can't trust you with my face sorry

OK

Are you from Nigeria

No problem

Promised

I will speak to you

But be honest

I'm Nigerian.

I will scam you guys forever

You people are full

I scam someone today 1000$

From USA

California

Fuck you

We made allot of money

Foolish woman

Fuck your ass

A military fake story and the coming out:

Iraq, South Sudan, and Pakistan...

I currently work with the US Special Forces Operational Detachment Team....Currently deployed to Kabul, Afghanistan

OK I understand

I had a very rough and tough childhood after my parents died. My family members and relatives abandoned me due to family vendettas and issues they had with my parents when they were alive, because they are no more...they had to pass the hatred towards me which them not to give a fuck about me and don't care to know or have anything to do with me and my family.....

But I hate people who lie

Okay, fine! You got me... I'm sorry I lied to you

So what happens now

Yes, you tell me who you are and we can speak

You are black, fine, no problem

From Nigeria?

Did you lose your voice

I am not the police ok

Well, yeah... I'm black and From Nigeria too

• • •

23

Military fake account on Instagram, real person is Jeff Sorensen [4], second face Philip 22 years old from Nigeria

 6   **113**   **158**
Beiträge   Abonn…   Abonni…

lames_rickie

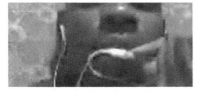

Some of the scammers work alone but most of them are part of so-called scammer groups like the *Yahoo Boys* in Nigeria or the *Illuminati* in Ghana. These groups are criminal groups and similar to the Mafia, with blood rituals and new members must swear, not to betray the group, but to serve the group. They sometimes live together in scammer houses in groups of around 10 people. The house is rented or the property of the chairman of the group. They work together and because of that the client often speaks to different people, depending on who is on duty. Phone numbers from all over the world mostly US, UK or Germany are used and the VPN Number of the computer is changed, so no one can locate, where they are really resident. Some also

---

[4] https://www.instagram.com/jeffreyyscott/?hl=de

work in Internet cafes, public places where a certain time is bought and used to scam people.

The phones used by scammers have always to be recharged with new credits because they use prepaid phones:

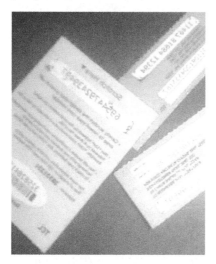

Some scammers are rich, they live in big houses with Jeeps in their garage. Others are very poor, not even having a bed, just sleeping on mattresses on the floor or without kitchen or bathroom.

The following examples show, what scammers want and what some of them really have.

There's my friend that met a American.... My wasn't making use of a fake profile, friend start dating this woman for a long time, the woman it Wealthy... One day my friend get to abeg her for just $1000 to start up a business and swear never to ask her for any favors.....to the woman $1000 is not a big deal but at the end she refused to help someone he called her boyfriend

Out of anger the guy was forced to join a scam, he added this woman with a fake profile, since then the woman has paid more that $50000

Now my question

● ● ●

This is how our kitchen looks like, my sister is actually cooking dinner

Outside view,,, you see the distance from my house

To get money from the clients, scammers both in Nigeria and in Ghana ask African magicians to do special money rituals to make the victim fall for them and send the money to them. For that they only need the full name of the client and a picture of the victim. Some even go to the country Benin to execute their rituals because there the magicians are *the best*. The victim is *charmed* and will start sending money to the fraud. Scammers also use magical rituals to protect themselves, to not fall for the client and not to be taken by the police. The worst rituals are done by the *Yahoo Plus* in Nigeria, but also by other groups: *human sacrifice*. Young women, babies or pregnant women are killed in order *to make the money come*. The magicians sometimes tell the frauds so wash with a special soap or to eat strange things to get the money flow started.

Here an example of an African magician on Facebook, offering his services:

I am THE GREAT BABA_olutude my brother and my sister God did not create any one to die in poor so don't sit down and die in poverty There are no side effects and no human sacrifice don't be afraid of anything have faith and call me now on (+2348145788306) when you are outside from Nigeria. I can help you online and don't say you have been try several times and failed remember all waters are the same but their different taste so you have to try and see I am here to help peoples out of their problems like
(1)instant money
(2)work of leadership
(3)money rituals
(4)business to move forward
(5)lotto number
(6)marriage problems
(7) promotion in work place
(8)luck of jobs

A scammer explaining, how money rituals work:

the pastor's preach the word of God to us from the Bible 15:17

I see 15:17

And traditional priests how do they celebrate 15:18

Well, traditional religion is a devil like religion whereby human or animal sacrifices are being made to idols 15:20

Let me say... Idol worship 15:20

Vodoo priest 15:21

Yeah, something like that 15:21

I understand 15:22

But over here, there are very powerful 15:22

Yes I imagine that 15:22

They can do all sort of things 15:22

Good and bad? 15:22

Yeah, something like that 15:21

I understand 15:22

But over here, there are very powerful 15:22

Yes I imagine that 15:22

They can do all sort of things 15:22

Good and bad? 15:22

Du
Good and bad?

Yeah, the bad is more than the good 15:27

Oh 😬 15:27

You have heard about money making rituals in Nigeria 15:27

I heard that some people do rituals to receive money 15:27

Yes 15:27

They can do all sort of things 15:22

Good and bad? 15:22

Du
Good and bad?

Yeah, the bad is more than the good 15:27

Oh 😬 15:27

You have heard about money making rituals in Nigeria 15:27

I heard that some people do rituals to receive money 15:27

Yes 15:27

Does this work 15:28

2 UNGELESENE NACHRICHTEN

Yes it works very well 15:33

But I can't do such 15:34

instead of going into money rituals... They decide to go into scamming 15:47

OK 15:47

Du
I once heard that the scammers take the picture of the Maga to the priest to make her or him pay

I won't lie to you,... Yes, there are scammers with alot if bad intentions 15:47

Alright, I understand 😄 15:48

Some scammers makes of vudoo power to scam people, and that kind of people are the once Making a lot of money with scamming 15:49

That's so bad 😥 15:49

Why nobody there tries to create something good for the young people 15:50

28

What 😊 15:43

Some are give some period of time to live and enjoy the money, after the time exhausted... They get to die 15:44

That is incredible 😊😊 15:45

I once heard that the scammers take the picture of the Maga to the priest to make her or him pay 15:46

Yeah, that's why many Nigerians, instead of going into money rituals... They decide to go into scamming 15:47

OK 15:47

> Du
> I once heard that the scammers take the picture of the Maga to the priest to make her or him pay

I won't lie to you,... Yes, there are scammers with alot if bad intentions 15:47

Because it has its side effects 15:34

OK which side effects 15:34

It depends on the vudoo priest 15:35

You mean the bad magic comes back to you 15:35

Or? 15:36

For example, you might do Money rituals with human sacrifice, and you start making money... Along the line you will be required to be making human sacrifice to that deity that made you rich...maybe once a month or once in six months 15:39

OK 15:40

And any day you fail to perform the human sacrifice, that day will be your end of existence 15:40

But that is very cruel 15:40

---

sacrifice, and you start making money... Along the line you will be required to be making human sacrifice to that deity that made you rich...maybe once a month or once in six months 15:39

OK 15:40

And any day you fail to perform the human sacrifice, that day will be your end of existence 15:40

But that is very cruel 15:40

The task for money making rituals differs, some gets to eat dry waste products like shit in form of a dog 15:42

What 😊 15:43

Some are give some period of time to live and enjoy the money, after the time exhausted... They get to die 15:44

That is incredible 😊😊 15:45

A lot of scammers take drugs, smoke weed and sleep with prostitutes. Some frauds even spend all their money on drugs and prostitutes.

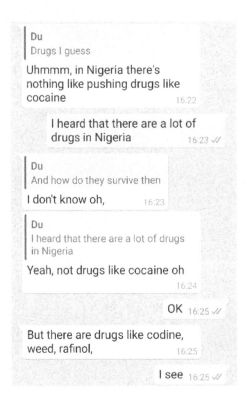

Du
Drugs I guess

Uhmmm, in Nigeria there's nothing like pushing drugs like cocaine   16:22

I heard that there are a lot of drugs in Nigeria   16:23 ✓✓

Du
And how do they survive then

I don't know oh,   16:23

Du
I heard that there are a lot of drugs in Nigeria

Yeah, not drugs like cocaine oh
                                        16:24

OK 16:25 ✓✓

But there are drugs like codine, weed, rafinol,   16:25

I see 16:25 ✓✓

I see 😊 15:51

And how could this change 15:51

In my state, instead of you to see something like factories, industries or companies that could create job employment..... Rather you will see hotel everywhere, promoting prostitution 15:53

Prostitution 😕 15:54

And who goes there 15:54

Every year, millions of students get to graduate from college with no means of employment 15:54

That's why Nigeria is really corrupt 15:55

I understand 15:55

But someone must change something 15:55

How will this end 15:55

bad culture, yeah 16:01

Yes, I believe you 16:01

But how could one create work there 16:02

By building factories, companies and industries 16:04

Anything you know that could employ people 16:04

And one thing I don't like is.... 16:05

If you should manage to get a job, the individual that is going to give that job to you would want you to sleep with him if you're a woman looking for that particular job 16:06

No 😨 16:06

If you are a man, they would want you to pay a huge amount of money for the job 16:06

I understand now 16:07

31

When the scammer has gotten the money from the Maga or Mugu, that is the victim, he will celebrate with his friends in a club with the stolen money, with champagne, with drugs and a lot of prostitutes. A prostitute costs around USD 20,- to USD 30,- in Ghana. Some scammers after having scammed the client call him or her on video to show the party going on and the money on the table, laughing at the victim!

Self-employed and non salary earners celebrate the purchase of new cars by throwing up cash in Benin, Edo State
Abingo S...

4. Different types of Formats used for Scam

4.1. Military Scam

Hello, I hope you had a nice restful sleep last night. I was really happy to chat with you on-line last night. After we chatted, I couldn't help but return to your profile and keep looking at your picture. I am really interested in getting to know you better, you seem to have the same values and commitment that I have. I just wish we lived closer so we can meet face to face, because it is so much easier to relate to someone when you can see in their eyes and see their physical reactions. So, tell me are you one that like to go out a lot or can just settle on staying home. I enjoy going out once in a while, but I also like to stay home with a good movie and some snuggling. In the summer I enjoy being at the beach, I love the ocean, either lying on the beach or going for walks and even bike riding. I also love music, dancing, music is my relaxer. What kind of food do you like? I enjoy steak, ribs, chicken, seafood, Chinese food. I love a good barbeque. You mentioned your age what month and date? We seem to have much in common, we both are looking for an honest, loving, loyal, respectful relationship. I am looking for that missing piece of my heart to fill. As we get to know each other more on-line, I do hope we will meet face to face. I awoke at 6am, unable to sleep I decided to write to you. Now it is 7:15AM and I need to get some more sleep. Have a great day! I will be anxiously waiting your email in return.

Hello, thanks so much for the mail you really make me happy and I will like to know you better. You are a very interesting woman and I really want to learn more about you. Will you give me a chance?...I want you to know that age means nothing in a relationship what matter most is our heart togetherness and the miles between us is just a number of place I believe we can work on it okay just let believe in the real love and heart sent from heaven above okay I believe everything will work out fine okay. Just let have faith in God I believe no one is perfect on earth. Thanks for your interest in me I am new to this online thing so please bear with me. I just wanted to drop you a line to let you know that I am interested in getting to know more about you after reading your profile. I guarantee that I am a nice man and know how to treat a woman...I'm an US army deployed oversea, currently in Farah, Afghanistan, I live in Susanville, CA Five years later my father was staying with my aunt in Arlington VA and my mom live in CA. My aunt told me that my father wasn't feeling well and was going to bed early. For some reason I woke at 4:00am the next morning and I drove in to check on him. When I arrived at the house, my aunt told me that father just has the flu. They had him buried in six inches of blankets and yet the bed was still shaking. he was burning up with fever. I rushed him to the hospital.

The doctors wanted to admit him but there wasn't a single bed available in the whole hospital. We waited 3 hours and finally a bed opened up in the intensive care unit for cardiac surgery. They had just finished hooking him up to the heart monitor when she experienced the first of seven heart attacks. He was at the only place in the whole world that had the technology to save him life. He spent the next six months in the hospital recovering and then came to live with my family another six months to regain his strength. He lived four more years before passing in 1995. I now know why I lost my job in 1995. It was a blessing. I do believe in a God. I believe that he guides us through life and helps us find our destiny. My dear I believe there is a reason we met. The sparkle in your eyes, pretty smile, and the warmth in your heart all make me happy. I am a real person with real feelings and I believe you are the same. I believe you to be an honest and caring person, it will be an honour to get to know you more. In your profile you seem to be a very down to earth woman and I really admire that! I guess I will leave you with this for now. I hope your day went well and I hope to hear from you soon. Thanks for reading this! I practically wrote you a book! Hehe! Let me know what you think about my pictures hope I don't scared you off lol.. Have a lovely Sunday and God bless you!

How are you doing, hope all is fine with you. Thanks so much for your reply you really make me happy to be honest with you. I really want to know you better if you don't mind. Pretty I have read your profile very well and I believe you imperfections are perfect to me so I believe we can both work things out all we need to do is just to have faith in God and I know things will work our based on believe, honest, trust and open-minded.

I want you to have faith in God that this our friendship will work out and leads us to something better in the future. Baby I want you to know that the age difference between us is just a number I don't care about it all I want you to know that is just a number it's what we can both work on it...How is your health which is most important to me...this are what am I like? I am 6ft:0 inch, black hair and black eyes...I am extraordinarily unique but with some average facets. I would enjoy watching while cuddled up on a couch with someone (especially if a cracking fire could be included).

To tell you little more about myself am a man bless with a lovely daughter name Sherry, I lost my son with my late wife some years ago on their way coming back from Russia in a plane crash 5 years ago, I'm Italian American but I was born and brought up in Italy and my mother is from Susanville, CA that where i live , a Average Body , mentally stable, physically fit, a bunch of laughs, warm, caring, honest, good listening, God Fearing, and a positive person. I am real easy person to talk to and a good listener.

I am sensitive, sentimental, compassionate, and caring, and can be moved to tears by something highly emotional. Life has thought me some hard lesson. Take the knowledge and wisdom I've gained and combine them with my personal qualities, and you have somebody who will someday be the best thing that ever happened to someone. The one who gains my affection will find me loyal, sincere and honest. Honesty is something I value highly, and when I have met people this way before, things have not gone beyond the first meeting if they turn out to have misrepresented them self in any way. I am here to broaden my opportunities to meet someone, but at the same time I am very content with where my life is now. I am not troubled by my past life. I hope to be in a good relationship would be icing on the cake....

I am an honest, trustworthy and kind hearten person and looking for someone that has the same values. I believe to build a relationship it takes a lot of work because am deaf since my parent dead and I believe you cannot do that seeing someone just once or twice a week and I like to spend a lot of time with the special person in my life. I do not play games and I am looking for someone with the same values and goals as myself. I have a saying and that is.... Life Is What You Make Of It. I will give it a shot! I am genius, passionate person, who tends to wear his heart on his shelve. I am romantic at heart, I believe that it is possible to have strong believes, and stay to true to yourself and still have fun and live life. I try to live my life being the best "me" I can be, improving as I go. I think one of the biggest gifts we are giving besides life itself is the gift of love and laughter and the biggest blessing we can find is someone who we can share our dreams with as friends, lovers, and partner in life together.

These letters show a so-called *format,* an instruction booklet, scammers use to make their victims fall for them. They just copy the text out of it and paste it to the client. They don't really speak to their victims. Usually while doing the *copy and paste game,* they watch TV or play video games. The military scammers often use Hangouts to chat. They usually don't call, saying that calls are not allowed at their base. In reality no real military men are looking for relationship on the Internet. They get enough salary; they have good food and they don't need help for any children. They are allowed to use Internet and do video calls. For a leave no fee has to be paid.

A common story military fakes use, is that they are widowers and have a child in the US or Europe in a boarding school. First, they make the victim fall in love and after a short time their child needs something. They connect the victim with the child on Hangouts. This child is the scammer himself writing like the following example shows:

Thanks so much Mom I'm so happy to hear from you Mom You know it have been long I called

*someone Mom, I'm so happy that I have someone I
can call Mom now Yes my Dad have told me a lot
about you, and I'm looking forward to be together
with you and my Dad as one family. Yes, Mom my
birthday is on Monday (12th) and I really want to
celebrate it. Mom my school is going for excursion
in Germany by the weekend so I want to celebrate
my birthday there in Germany with my friends Mom.
Mom, I'm really sad that you and my Dad are not
going to be there to celebrate it with me. Mom I just
need you and Dad to support so that I can celebrate
it with my friends there in Germany Mom I will be
glad if you and Dad help me with this okay I'm so
much Happy to have you as my Mom and I know
that you are going to be a good Mom to me and
going to be a good son too Mom.*

The contact with the fake child continues and he or
she will always need something and the victim pays
because in the meantime the scammer has asked
her to become his *wife*, so she feels responsible for
the poor child.

Also, the fake military man is in troubles in the
meantime and needs maybe to pay for hospital
treatment.

Honey i'm already crying right now because am going to miss you and i don't really know how that is, i don't even know how am going to be communicating with you my love

Baby after two days and you didn't hear from me just know that I'm no more

Ok I cannot change the situation, I must take it as it is. But I am not happy

↓ Zur Neuesten

I thank God i returned safely

But was injured

Oh what happened?

Now I take aid into clinical base here in Iraq

I see

There

a very big problem on this

↓ Zur Neuesten

goodness i finally did it

Another popular trick is the one with the box to be sent to the client. She or he then will have to pay high fees for the receipt of the box. The box never arrives and the money is gone.

40

As we confronted and finally took over the terrorists hide-out; to my greatest surprise, during our raiding and bursting, we found lots of ammunition and lots of dangerous nuclear weapons in the cave.

We also found some precious Treasures and Suitcases filled with Cash.

Ok

It is unbelievable

Ok

we counted the money and shared it among ourselves. my own share of it is $2.1 million dollars

The secret is that only few of us know about the money, and we are not willing to surrender it to the government.

You cannot keep this money, it is not yours

Jetzt

↓ Zur Neuesten

41

i couldn't deposit the money into my account. The Government has banned the Banks from working here because of the on going war. Banks are restricted from working for security reasons

Others who shared from the cash have already sent theirs at once to their families or loved ones to keep for them and I am swiftly advised to do the same

But I really don't have someone to send this kind of cash to. It is too urgent for me. My heart has been so bittered because i may lose the money if i fail to remove the box that contains my money

I see

from their custody before the deadline. I worked so hard for this money and i can't afford to lose it.

Jetzt

A couple of days ago, i got an email from the security company where i kept the package that contains my money

Ok

letting me know that the date for me move this package out from their custody is 24 SEP 2019 which is very difficult for me to do at this time.

Jetzt

from their custody before the deadline. I worked so hard for this money and i can't afford to lose it.

I had planned to go into investment with this money after my retirement.

Ok

You know I am coming to you so we can invest together

Jetzt

..

If the Inspection Team come around and find it, it will be confiscated.

> And why do you tell me all this

Because I know you can help me out

so i kept the money inside a small safe box for the time being and left it with one of the security company over here.

Jetzt

together

I know we haven't met. but my heart tells me that i can trust you.

> No you cannot

> Because I know who you are

> You scam women and me

What do you mean

> And now you want me to wash your dirty money

Honey, am so happy to hear from you, I was wondering if you are really OK and I have been missing you my love, I woke up very wet this morning, cos I dreamed of you making love to me, and when I woke up, I found out it was just a dream, wow!!! I was damn wet in my panties love, and I wished I could continue my dream. LOL, lol, god I am really in love with you my dearest Freddie. Anyways am so glad you are fine, I will be with you soon my love, and we will make awesome love together. Am so glad you are fine, my heart beat for you all second of all day. Yes, we are more than lovers now, we are couple, we are to be married soon, maybe in Las Vegas, if you make me your lovely wedded wife, I will be very, very glad my love.

43

Sweetheart like I said, I am very, very surprised to hear that the shipping company needed another money before they could deliver to you the box, this is a delay towards getting the box to you love. Honey, this will never separate us my love, it will never make me be upset with you or the company, I understand they are doing their job. Honey, is not your fault that the package is out there now, but love we must do something before is too late love, honey all am doing is for us, I shipped this thing cos here is no more safe to keep such high valuables, and for you to know I love and trusted you with my life savings and my documents, and for our future use. But now if we leave the box out there, cos of 680 we are making a big mistake, cos what is in those boxes can never be compared to 680.

Honey, I have also received email from Col. Rose as well, she explained all she went through to make sure she get the boxes registered, but eventually the cash I gave her wasn't enough and she was shot of cash, she said that she even made few expenses for us from her own cash. Honey, I guess she just tried.

Baby the box is not wooden box, it is a brown metallic box, highly sophisticated, it is secured with security codes, which i have given you, when you receive the box, you will unlock them, and take more than 680 my love., But hun, Col. Rose wrote in her email that the shipping company have to put the box in a wooden grates to secure it from damaging, maybe all these makes their charges high i guess, and the box have to be registered as a highly classified package cos the total money in them is 1.2m USD, with my military documents. Baby am not happy that 680 USD is hanging the boxes out there, is making me feel bad now, but am not upset with you my love.

Baby right now I can't do anything from here, we can't send out any money from this place, and I have to put all my money in those box with hope that there won't be any other need for expenses concerning the box, and here is just a war zone and a Muslim country, is not save for us here, and they don't allow us to go make transactions. and I don't have a Muslim friend who can help us, even when we get one, we can't trust them, all these crisis here is among the reasons I decided to ship my belongings to you love, and to prove to you how much I love u and want us to be happy together. So honey, you have to try my love. please love just try get the boxes home with you, 680 cannot be compared to what is in the box, so my love just get the box out and you will replace the 680 wherever you get it OK, even if it will require getting a loan, just do it honey, we can't afford to allow the box out there, these are what I have suffered for, and all i hope to settle down with any man that will love me and cherish me, which I have come to believe that man is you Augustine. So am spending my life time with you love. Honey, just follow the shipment company instructions and get home the box, so that we will have enough money to spend when I come home, to live a perfect life I been dreaming of.

Honey, I want u to look for a good car too, I like Benz cars, like CLK or Chevy cars, but you can also go for the ones you like, cos your wish comes first OK and also look for a good house to buy for us, we need to live a charming life my love, but this will be when you get the box home OK!!!.

Baby please you got to understand that here they don't operate like we do there in the States, and we are in a war here. So, honey, u got to do whatever you can to complete the remaining balance of 680 which you said they requested, so that they can ship you the boxes. I think you need to contact the delivery Company to get info on how to pay the 680 left, so that they will deliver to you our boxes ASAP.

I love you with all my heart and soul, and I dream of a day when you will ask me to be your lovely wife, and that day I hope we be full of love making for us love, lol.

Another popular scam is the one with the *military leaving form*. The victim will receive fake papers from US Army like this, asking him or her to pay for the military man to leave.

UNITED STATES OF AMERICA JOINT FORCE WITH NORTH ATLANTIC TREATY ORGANIZATION – NATO- PEACE KEEPING CAMP BASE ABUJA NIGERIA, UNITED STATES MILITARY INTERNATIONAL LEAVE BOARD. Attention: Madam XXX EMERGENCY LEAVE APPLICATION FOR SERGEANT ADAMS WAYNET his is to acknowledge the receipt of leave Application made on behalf of your fiancé Williams arias a US troop on peace keeping mission, terrorism confidential mission, here in Abuja Nigeria, under my command and military jurisdiction. I understand through this application and the previous discussions with her on her affairs and marriage proposal to you and that she is to proceed for a marital arrangement with you and has so much talked on this matter and seeks now to conclude with you to be his legal husband. I must inform you here that she is of an important mission holding a profound position in security and monitoring duties as one of our military intelligence here. And the only martial commandant we have here in the camp Accordingly, you should also note that this is not time for his official leave but not withstanding she will be granted an emergency leave in other for her to get to your country to get a finalizations for marriage with you.. I must also bring to your notice that the United States military authority does not ask our troops to pay for their official leaves or holidays/vacations assigned and approved by the military authority but in a situation where any *member of the US army on his or her own discretions and agreement with his fiancé apply or request for an emergency leave it must involve payment of fees in line with the number of weeks or months leave duration will be chosen as available for only emergency reasons on request by troops on peace keeping mission only. NOTE: the payment involves payment for his flight, because she will be coming home to you through the military flight, and also the flight will head straight to US for her replacement. And you to have it in mind that her salary will be sent to her immediately she gets to your country safely. It is very important that you understand these points very well and the more reasons you must pay and support in other to give this office the support to give approval to your request to have her home only for marital reasons. We have the following leave durations to be considered and approved for accepted Applicants seeking for coming home of their fiancé on peace keeping mission and as I have offered you the chance to choose from the below leave durations with non-negotiable payments attached to each leave duration. The United States military officers seeking for emergency leave to fulfil marital proposal and promises are entitled for the following leave/ emergency vacation options as stated below and must use it as requested and no misconduct is to be tolerated: EMERGENCY LEAVE CATEGORIES(A) 8 WEEKS LEAVE DURATION: $650.00 USD(B) 16 WEEKS LEAVE DURATION:*

$820.00 USD(C) SIX MONTHS (HONEY MOON) LEAVE DURATION: $1,350.00 USD. The above leave Durations are made available for you to choose and send payment according to choice made for your fiancé depending on your capability and expected time that you will want her to spend with you. The reasons of payment for emergency leave Application is to assist the US military authority in replacement expenses and supporting of troops coming to take over duties from any one going on emergency leave and must be considered worthy and a way of ensuring that our troops are protected and allowed to judiciously make use of their times for reasons they are applied and paid for. This must be well understood for any applicant/fiancé, and instructions made herein must be dully followed with the payment of the amount fixed on each emergency vacation choice made in accordance of the rules and all guidelines clearly stated on this memo to avoid mistake or termination of approval. PAYMENT INFORMATION TO BE TAKEN TO WESTERN UNION MONEY TRANSFER AGENT:NOTE: THAT PAYMENT SHOULD BE DEPOSITED DIRECTLY TO OUR REGIONAL OFFICE IN ABUJA NIGERIA - WHERE YOUR WIFE IS PRESENTLY DEPLOYED, ON A CONFIDENTIAL TERRORISM MISSION ONLY THE PAYMENT INFORMATION BELOW SHOULD BE TAKEN TO THE WESTERN UNION MONEY TRANSFER AGENT TO SEND THE DURATION OF LEAVE / VOCATION YOU HAVE

CHOSEN.NAME OF SENDER………………………………..AMOUNT TO SEND………………………………………LOCATION OF RECEIVER …………………………… 82 DIVISION ENUGU_NIGERIANAME OF RECEIVER…………….. NWANEVU UGONNATEXT QUESTION………………. WHAT FORANSWER……………………. vacation MONEY TRANSFER CONTROL NUMBER (MTCN)…………………….NOTE: ONCE YOU MAKE THE PAYMENT YOU SEND TO US A COPY OF THE PAYMENT INFORMATION THROUGH EMAIL.NOTE: For any choice you have made from the above leave durations, payment must be made in full within 7 days from today either in full or part of the fee to get his name fixed on the vacation list on time and to avoid mistakes or miscalculations in replacement expenses as explained above. Thank you! Best Regards. CAPTAIN NWANEVU UGONNA.UNITED STATES INTERNATIONAL LEAVE BOARDANNEX ABUJA UNIT NIGERIA PEACE

If the woman wants to see *her future husband,* she has to pay a certain amount. Possible is also that she gets a fake call from a fake officer from US army, asking her if she will pay for the leave of *her man.* The man of course never arrives at her home and the money is lost.

4.2. Real Estate Scam

Some scammers use the real estate scam, telling their victim to transfer a lot of money to them to buy the new home for the future together. The woman will receive fake papers from a fake lawyer, maybe also fake calls, where she is asked to transfer the money. All these papers are faked and the house to be bought does not exist in reality. The money is gone, the heart is broken. Some people lose everything and even take loans to fulfil the future dream of a new home and marriage, not knowing that this person is a fake person. The only thing he or she wants is money. When the money of the victim is finished, the scammer disappears in the darkness of the Internet. There are people who, after all this, commit suicide. The scammer does not care about that, he is already speaking with the next client.

4.3. Fake Accidents or Fake with ill Relatives

There are also scams executed with fake accidents or ill relatives in need to be operated to save their lives. The victim is set under pressure, everything has to be done very quickly, so she will not have enough time to think about it. If she doesn't pay the other one will die and that is then her fault. Some receive fake calls from fake doctors in the hospital, telling that the beloved person needs to be operated quickly, it's about life and death and who will pay the bill for the operation. Or a sister is in need of a transplantation that costs USD 20.0000. She will die if she doesn't get the transplantation. A fake call is done where the victim speaks to the ill relative. In reality no one is ill. This story is just used to get money from the client. Sometimes the bank account of the hospital is given to the client to transfer the money for the operation or treatment there, in reality this account is from a *drop,* someone who is working for the scammer and who then passes on the money to him.

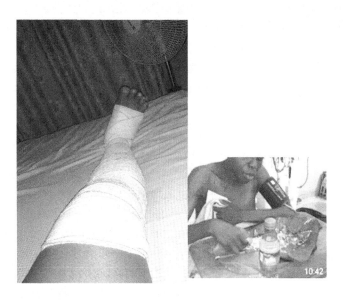

To Whom It May Concern......

Good day madam, I am Dr XXX from Sesan Hospital Lagos Nigeria. I am written you in respect of an accident victims in our hospital who are foreigner in this country. He is Mr D. A. and he is with a little boy of about 7 to 8 years old .... I got your contact from his diary as his wife to be. I am very sorry to inform you that your husband is laying down critically unconscious in the hospital after he and a little boy were rushed down to our hospital on Thursday evening at about 21 hour GMT by members of the red cross of Nigeria involving in a car accident on their way to the airport. Presently he and the little boy are unconscious and not responding to treatment. We have tried to put them on a live saving machine till the both of them are awake. Madam, I would want you to contact the hospital management because I have been told no treatment should be given out to them until someone who knows them is identified with them and a deposit of $900 is paid to allow us to commence treatment.

Madam, I want you to know that Mr X has a severe internal bleeding and has broken his legs but the boy is only unconscious with little injury. please madam I am afraid that they may lose their lives if something is not done on time to rescue the situation at hand. you can contact the hospital management as soon as possible to identify yourself as the man's wife. I want you to know that if we can take a quick step, we can save their lives and they will be back on their feet again.

please madam treat this with urgency and get back to the hospital management via this email r.sesanhospital@gmail.com or on our phone number +234xxxxxxx , please get back to us as soon as possible because this is an urgent matter OK Madam ...

Good morning my love .. I hope you had a sweet night and dream about us my love. How is our daughter, Wendy doing? Honey, this morning I had to rush our son, Ray to the nearest hospital my love, he was complaining of pain in his abdomen and I had to rush him to the hospital .. when we got here the doctor diagnosed him and told me that our son had APPENDICITIS and that it has shown classic symptoms on him and that they need to carry out an abdominal surgery on him before the appendix burst and that can lead to a great effect on our son my love .. Honey, the doctor said this disease sometimes happen to kids of his age and its normal to do an abdominal surgery for them and remove the appendix .. and he said our bill to make the surgery and other necessary treatment for him is $950. Honey, I'm so confused right now and I don't know what we will do my love. Honey, if only we could get someone to give us a loan and we would pay up as soon as this company pays my money in few weeks time .. I have already ask Mr Wale for his help but he seems to be having a family problem as *well .. Honey, I'm so confused and scared I pray that we are able to get the money soon so that the appendix will not burst inside him my love. He's being given injection to reduce the pain until we pay them the money for the surgery my love .. Right now, I am lying beside our son at the hospital and I'm able to write you with one of their computers here my love ... I love you honey, hope to hear from you soon ..*

Good morning my love. I hope your fine honey .. Honey, something terrible happened this morning my love .. I don't really want to tell you about it but I have tried my best to solve it alone but my best is not working .. Our son just collapsed this morning and I called for help and we had to rush him to the hospital .. Immediately the doctor diagnosed him and told me that Ray is in a critical condition and it's because he doesn't feed well as before, though he was having high temperature last night but I never thought it could be this worse my love .. The doctor has put him on a live saving machine and he's been giving some oxygen to revive his life before the normal treatment is been done on him .. The doctor told me that they really need to act fast in treating our son and that we need to make a deposit of $950 which Mr Wale did paid $50 and that makes them to still put our son on the live saving machine my love .. The doctor gave us 24 hours to get the remaining $900 paid or else he's gonna remove the live saving machine from him and anything bad can happen if *he does that .. Honey, our son is dying my love, I am so scared now and I don't know what to do .. I have tried to talk to Mr Wale and he told me that he doesn't have more than the $50 he gave to the hospital and I also tried the business man cell number but it's not going through yet my love .. Honey, I didn't wish to let you know cos I thought I could solve it myself but now I can't solve it myself any longer .. Honey, we have to act fast on this my love, I know you don't have much money on you too but please our son's life is at stake .. I am writing you from the hospital now my love .. Honey, I want you to please come and take our son home after he survived this incident ok my love and he could receive good care with you .. I am so scared right now my love, I don't wanna lose our son honey ....*

4.4. Different Scams with Payments

Another popular trick is the scam with different payments like the fake bail after arrest. The victim receives a fake call from the police, telling her that the beloved man has been arrested and a bail has to be paid to set him free. Or his documents were stolen, he is in Africa without passport and needs money for that. Or his money was stolen and he can't pay the hotel bill etc.

Honey, I am sad with very depressed heart and crying face. I am really hurting; I am having another serious problem right now my love and I am scared *coz I don't ever want to lose you.... Honey, I hope you will understand and see reason that it's never my fault to bring this to you. Honey, when we got to the airport last night, we were checked and our traveling documents were checked and they detected in our passport that we have stayed longer than we should here and it's a great offense and I was apprehended by the immigration officers, they said Ray is just a kid and that it's me they will deal with. They have even seized my passport and they are going to charge me to court which I could go to jail. Honey, I am sorry that this is happening to us and I want you to know that I never wished for this to happen my love. I told them all I have gone through but they are not willing to hear me out. They said its either I go to jail or I pay a fine of $7,500...that's the rule. Honey I know you have always been there for our family and now I need you more than ever OK my love, I need you to help me build my faith and make me strong OK honey cos now I feel very insecure and I feel so sad my love. I am even thinking of killing myself coz I feel like my life is doomed and cursed, I don't even know. But I talked to Mr Wale and he said he will help us with a room in his hotel so me and Ray can stay there free until I am able to get the money for the immigration. Honey, I know you have really done so much for our family and you are the most wonderful mother and wife in the world. Honey, I don't want to bother you with this problem OK my love cos I know you still have some bills to pay up* *too. but I am thinking on how to figure a way out so I can get the money and pay it to them. I know you will feel so sad about this my love but please don't hurt yourself OK my love ...I need you so much, please understand that it's not my fault OK honey, all this just seems to be coincident. I miss you my dear wife. Feeling so sad right now my love.*

Hello sweetheart How are u doing my love? I have really missed u so much sweetie and still can't wait to meet u hun...Well I really have a Problem here my love and can u believe I have not eaten for the past four days, I really don't want u to know about this before but I realise I don't have any choice than to let u the woman I want to be with forever know my problems....I lost my wallet and my credit card and I have nothing on me am really hungry here babe...I need your help sweetie I just need 550$ for now so when I get my Pay check I will return it for u okay.. Hope to hear from u soon

Good morning my love, honey I am having a little problem with my hotel bills, well I was just informed by the hotel management that my bills has expired and I have to pay up immediately, I tried to pay the bill with my credit card but the machine rejected my credit card, I called the hotel manager and explain things to him , he told me I should call my bank to inform them, in which I did that but I was told that my credit card has been hacked by hacker and that the only way is for me to come back home before I can have access to it. and you know that I have few days to complete my work my dear and I have to pay before I leave the hotel, I want you do me a big favour.... I know that this will be hard for you to do ,honey I really need your help on these, if you can loan me some amount of money($650) to pay my hotel bills I will really appreciate it and I promise I will pay back as soon as I get access to my credit card.....I'm so ashamed that I am doing this, I have never done this or experienced these in my life .....Honey I am counting on you please don't let me down......please its urgent. I love you

Hi Sweetie, how are you doing, I am emailing you to let you know that I just confirm my flight details. but there's something bothering me now. I know you would be thinking I should be on my way home now. Baby I have been here thinking about you here as well. You are always in my heart also in my thought every single seconds of my life. You mean a lot in my life because you amazed me so much. I promise am not going to make you regret doing all this and trying to give me a happy face.. You will be that person I would always see and smile because you are so awesome. I have been thinking here and I don't know what am going to do now, I know you only give me a chance to see what's going to happen ,I would really love to meet you myself but I am so confused why life has been so Unfair to me. I was informed by a ticket agency here that I will need to show up some money at the board pass before I will be allowed to fly out of the country...

The money is called (International Travelling Allowance) and it is REFUNDABLE though they will not take it from me. it's just to show up at the board pass in other for them to be sure that I have a sufficient funds for my trip. said its one of their new rules here and they are doing it for the safety of people. I told them that America is where I live and I was just here for some reason but they said it's the normal procedure, concerning the new national rules. When I was told this, I was so sad and depress and I almost gone crazy because I never wanted to bother you again after all you have done for me. Never knew how to tell you this because all I was expecting to tell you in our next chat was about my schedule. You everything in my life and I am sorry I had to take you through this rough road but I promise to make it worth your while. Just got out of some little issues and now this. I am really sorry for taking you through this rough road. I still don't have any option than getting the fund. Sweetie, I don't really know what exactly to do now. I don't want to lose you because you have been an angel sent from above down to me, I just want to appreciate all you have done for me but got another weak side. I am going to be with you NO MATTER WHAT after I get out of this unknown place. I am really sorry about this. I will just need to show up this money for a confirmation at the board pass and they will give it back to me once they confirm it and then I will be allowed to board my flight. the money is not for spending and I will bring the money back home and *you will have it back immediately I arrive baby ...I hope you understand this honey and I will be very much happy for you to assist me out with as soon as possible so that i can get things done ready for my trip.. I await you swift response. Remember, I told you it is REFUNDABLE. I am bringing it back to you. The money is $3500. I honestly don't wish for this. I just hope you'd understand how sad this is for me. I am really sorry that this is happening, wish I could help it and not bug you like this and now I am very ashamed of myself and I am scared of losing you. I couldn't even tell Ray yet. Baby, please ...*

Honey, how are you doing today my love? I have been thinking about you all day and I missed you so much. Honey I am writing you to let you know about some progress that is coming our way now my love. Honey, I talked to the lawyer about the balance I ought to receive from the company I worked for here cos they refused to pay me my balance ..though our agreement was that they will pay it to my credit card account when I get back home to the states.. The company told me that there is no way they can pay me while I am still here and that they can only pay it to my account when I get back home to the states. But fortunately for us my love, I talked to the lawyer about it and he said there is a way he would make the company pay, not to me here but to you, my wife .... and that we will pay him a sum of $1000 before he commence the work and he assured me that the company will transfer the

money to your credit card account my love
...Sweetheart, I need you to help me get the money
from the company since I am not in the states right
now. As you know honey, you are my other half, my
wife and you are the only one I have... so I trust you
to handle it perfectly for me my love. Really, I can't
get it because I am not in the states and its been
part of our agreement, they can't send the money
down here in Africa. Sweetheart, this is an
opportunity for us and a way out ok my love. Honey
all we need now is the money to pay the lawyer and
your credit card info so they can make the transfer
of the money as soon as the lawyer finishes his
work... Honey, I need all the info on the card, I
mean all the info used in opening the cc account. As
soon as the lawyer does his work and you give the
cc info to me, the transaction will be made and all
will be well with us and our family will be together
forever. All the loan we have received will be paid
ok my love ... We've been through a lot together and
we deserve to be happy and that's what I believe so
much, we are going to become very happy for the
rest of our lives. I know and understand perfectly
well that things are kind of rough and tough but it's
said that when the going gets tough, then the tough
get going. Our love is very much stronger than this
little time trials and we are gonna overcome all
obstacles. Honey, I wanna thank you for your love
and support on our family ...I really appreciate it and
i am grateful and i also promise to make you happy
for the rest of your life and also, you 'll never for

once have a cause to be sad about ever meeting or knowing me. That, I promise...love you so much my love and I'll be waiting for your response earnest ok honey... God bless our family, you, Wendy, Ray, me, your mom and our future kids. I love you my dear wife.

Honey, how have you been? I have been thinking about you all day and I missed you so much. Honey I am writing you to let you know about some progress there is with me now. I am about to get my balance of the contract I came here to do from the people I took the contract from. Sweetheart, I need you to help me get it from them since I am not in the states right now. As you know, you are my other half and you are the only one I have so I trust you to handle it perfectly for me. I can't get it because I am not in the States and its been part of our agreement. They can't send money down here in Africa. Sweetheart, please give me your cc info so they can make the transfer right away ok. Honey, I need it as soon as possible so I can get my money from them ok. Sweetie, I need all the info on the card, I mean all the info used in opening the cc account. As soon as you give that to me, the transaction will be made and all will be well with us and we would be able to start our new life without stress. We have been through a lot together and we deserve to be happy and that's what I believe so much, we are gonna become very happy for the rest of our lives. I know and understand perfectly well that things are a kind of rough and tough but it's said that when the going gets tough then the tough get going. Our love is very much stronger than this little time trials and we are gonna overcome all obstacles. Honey, I wanna thank you for being and staying with me. I really appreciate it and I am grateful and I also promise to make you happy for the rest of your life and also, you will never for once have a cause to be sad about ever meeting or knowing me. That I promise...love you so much my baby and I will be waiting for your response earnest ok.

Good morning my love .. sorry I didn't pick up your call last night, I slept off early ok my love. Honey , there is a good news for us this morning , Mr wale just loan me a sum of $3000 this morning , though he said he wanted to loan me the whole $6000 to pay up the Immigration money but that was all he was able to get for us my love ... yesterday , me and Mr wale with the lawyer went to the company to ask if they will still pay by the end of the month but the MD told us that the management of the company will have to follow the agreement that was made before by me and the company . I felt very sad and asked our lawyer if there is something he could do but he said he doesn't have the privilege to sue the company since that was our previous agreement .. this was the reason why Mr wale tried all he could to get us the money this morning cos he knows the way I feel about all this mess and he knows I'm tired of this place my love ... Now, the company has *agreed to pay me when I get back home to the states and the lawyer is monitoring that .. but the most important thing for me is to get home and see my family and however, I would make my credit card starts working as soon as I get back home and send Mr wale his own money even before the company pays the money .... Honey, I have check every necessary thing that me and Ray needs to get home and I have confirmed that my documents are intact and good, just the complete $6000 and we are home my love .. Honey, I am thinking that I could get $1000 by selling some of my shoes and the remaining of my suit but I'll keep just one suit when coming back home .. Honey , I know what we have been through together and I know that you don't have much money with you but please try all you can to get us the remaining $2000 ok my love , i know this will be hard for you but let's both try our best and put an end to all this problem ok my love .. I pray that our lord will help us and make us get the complete money soon my love ... me and Ray are tired of being held here and I just want to be home and make my credit card starts working then I could pay back all I have loan from you and from Mr Wale and we could also pay Barbie her money too ... Honey , i want to be home soon my love , if not this week , then latest next week .. I want to touch and hold you my dear wife and also hold our daughter, Wendy .. and say thank you to your mom for her love too and meet with the rest of the family .. I am totally tired of being here and I hope you understand* *that my love .. I love you honey and I love our kids too my love*

Honey, I hope you are having a great day at work today my love .. Me and Ray did played some games in the afternoon time and we went for swimming later in the day my love .. Honey, we both miss you all day my dear wife .. Honey, the immigration officer came to the hotel today and we talked .. He came with some documents of the immigration cards he has done for people and he also showed me other identity of his and he assured me that he would do the immigration card as soon as we are ready and that i should put trust in him .. I told him about the money we paid earlier and that the receipt got lost somehow, and he said that money we paid then is not reflected in the record since we did not pay it at a time. He said if I should go direct to the office again, I would be asked to pay another $7500 since that previous one doesn't reflect .. He said he has helped a lot of people in this same situation as mine and that Me and my son would get home soon if we are able to pay him .... He said we should pay the sum of $1500 and everything will be done in few days from now but I told him that I don't have up to that, and that he should please help me and my son .. After I have pleaded with him for a while, he then told me that he would consider me due to the trouble I have been through .. He said he would collect the sum of $1200 , and that he would collect $800 now and *when he finish , he would collect the balance of $400 and I asked him if I could pay him the remaining $400 after me and my son gets home to the states and he said its ok by him that he trust me and he knows that I am a good man ... Honey, I would suggest maybe we should pay Barbie half of her money first ok my love and we would pay the other half when me and Ray gets home .. Honey, I have been praying all day and i know our lord will bring me and Ray home safely .. Honey, when will you receive the tax payback money my love? I hope it will be soon so that all this bad dream would be over once and for all ... Take good care of yourself and have a wonderful day my love .. I'll be looking forward to your call when you get back from work ..*

4.5. Invitations

Some scammers, mostly after they have admitted to be black, ask for *an invitation*. This form of scam is often used to get money for the flight ticket and other things like to buy a suitcase etc. Some scammers want to get out of their country, so they really come to the country of the victim and maybe some really marry him or her. There is different evidence on that, some relationships work, others not. After a certain time, the *ex-scammer* maybe leaves the *ex-victim* and takes a different partner, mostly a younger one. There are also white women who go to Nigeria or Ghana to meet the scammers and spend some time with them there. This is not recommendable because it is very dangerous! These are criminal elements and therefore everything can happen to the white person.

4.6 AT&T Scam

Another form of scam, mostly in the US, is the so-called AT&T scam. It is the world's largest telecommunications company, the largest provider of mobile telephone services and the largest provider of fixed telephone services in the United States. The client is contacted via phone by the scammer, trying to get personal information like birth date, address, social security number, credit card number etc. Once the scammer has the information, all the personal data are used to do shopping transactions on the Internet or other Internet abuse.

4.7. Bank Details Collection

Frauds try to get bank information from the client. They use the collected data to shop online, to send parcels to the client, asking him or her to pass these on to another address. Some scammers also send *gifts* to the victim: gold, silver, rings, flowers, food, clothes to convince the client that they *really love him or her.*

Some scammers ask the client to establish a bank account to send money there. The client is then asked to pass this money on to another account, not knowing that this is money laundry and therefore a crime. There are cases, where clients out of love for the scammer did this and went to prison.

Hey honey how you doing sorry I didn't talk to you all day, I was in duty all day, well I got a message from the head office today, that our allowance and family care money will be paid to our relatives by next week, that we should provide, that we should provide out beneficiary info, address and bank account or cc details for the money, because the state military is not going to issue any cheque out to any beneficiary if he or she don't have an account, and the beneficiary most be 18yrs above, my only son is ten years old and my grandma is too old to start going around for this, so baby I want to trust you with this I want you to help me get the money to your account or get a credit card that can receive this money soon, the information that will be needed for this transaction is.....

Full name

Address

Date of birth

Occupation

Sex

Bank name

Routine number

Online access

Username

Password

Email address

Email password

Account security question and answers

but if you can't get all of that you can get Wallsfargo days pay card, chase liquid card or capital one cc

Love you so much honey, I will be glad if you help me with this and you can take from the money once it gets to you

4.8. Lottery and Bitcoin Scam

Some scammers work with the lottery or Bitcoin scam.

This is my new Facebook profile I had trojan virus on my laptop and it destroyed my account.so add this new one and delete the old one Am fine, just busy online Searching on what to invest my Grant

Money on and you? Good...Have you heard about the federal government grant?

This is specifically place for those who need assistance paying for bills, buying a home, starting their own business, going to school, or even helping raise their children with old and retired people. This is a new program, I got $90,000 delivered to me when I applied for the grant and you don't have to pay it back.. you can also apply too. Once you click on this link https://www.facebook.com/XXX/about it will lead you to the agent Facebook page just send him a friend request then message him that you want to claim for the Grant and let me know when you do that, so I can put you through.

Once you text the agent on this # (949) XXX that you want to claim for the Grant and let me know when you do that, so I can put you through. When you contact the agent, he will have to check on their automated data base system if you are among the randomly selected people who can get a Grant and then proceed to some other processes and have your info and you will choose your Grant option and will have to pay for the clearance of your file (case fee, file fee, label fee and shipping fee) and once the cashier gets it and process your Grants documents and certificates your Grant will be delivered to you the next day after the confirmation by their UPS agent. I was told to pay for clearance fee before the UPS can Deliver my Grant Money I choose 90,000 and the charges was 2000 that all I did to get my Grant Money

It is real, when a sister's friend of mine told me about it I was scared and wondered if something that could be this true would be real, and I contacted the agent and qualified and got my Grant money delivered to me after I passed all the process The Grant is from the office of the Federal Reserve conjunction with IMF and UNICEF to serve as an economic aid to all... I mean a legitimate government employee or representative of the Federal government will not hesitate to provide a link to information concerning their agency's purpose. It was the UPS agent that brought it for me after I qualified. You will have to go through a series of processes to check if you qualify and once you qualify the agent will also tell you what next to do....It is not like they will just give everyone a Grant.... They have an automated database that has saved everyone's information. Once he checks and sees you qualified he will take you through the process It was sent to me through a certified mail check from the headquarters through UPS... And I took it to bank immediately to verify if it was real and legit.. And bank confirmed to me that it was real He is the claim agent in charge of registering and distributing Grants. He's the agent in charge

AGENT...

Hello

What can I do for you? How did you get on my private Facebook page? I can help you to get the grant as soon as you are honest with me. Hope you have a good credit record? No or yes by client, continue you we help him or her out to get it. You have to fill up some information's so we can proceed: OH OKAY, HOLD LET ME CHECK IF YOUR PROFILE NAME IS STILL AVAILABLE ON OUR GRANT LIST DATABASE. Give me your full name to check if your name is on our Data Base Hold let me check if your name is still available on our Data Base Congratulation on your grant as our verification team alerts that your data verification process was successful.

I will need to confirm some information before we can deliver your grants to you in your home, the grants will be delivered to you as soon as the information required are duly filled:

Full name........

Address......

Male/Female ....

Age.....

Married/Single.....

Text or Phone Number.......

E-mail........

Hearing or Deaf.......

Do you Own a house or Rent Appt........

Do you want cash or check?

A valid copy of ID.....

Your application was forwarded to delivery department after the due processing by the administrative department, it shows that you are qualify to receive the grant and your Grants has been confirmed and the money will be delivered to you in next 24hours in Check. We will like to let you know that the money is tax free and you don't have to pay taxes on the Federal Government Grant. A certificate will be issue to you at the point of delivery showing and telling you the money is tax free so you don't need to pay taxes. We have verified your information's and it shows that you are qualify to receive the grant, you are to choose the amount you wish to claim from us, and you will pay for the Clearance fees. We will make every effort to ship your order

You Pay $5,000 and get $50,000,00.

You pay $6,000 and get $90,000,00.

You pay 7,000 and get $150,000,00.

You pay $8,000 and get $200,000.00

You pay $9,000 and get $300,000.00

You pay $10,000 and get $450,000.00

You pay $11,000and get $550,000.00

You pay $12,200 and get $750,000.00

Final you pay $13,000 get $1,000,000.00

You pay $1,000 and get $50,000,00.

You pay $2,000 and get $90,000,00.

You pay $3,000 and get $100,000,00.

You pay $4,000 and get $150,000,00.

You pay $5,000 and get $200,000.00

You pay $6,000 and get $300,000.00

You pay $7,000 and get $450,000.00

You pay $8,000 and get $550,000.00

You pay $9,200 and get $750,000.00

Final you pay $12,000 get $1,000,000.00

As soon as the payment is facilitated through Western Union or Money Gram to our office your Grant Money will be delivered to you the next 24 hours. Let us know when you are ready so that we can give you the details you are to send to through western Union or Money Gram Store. One more thing....Don't disclose your winning to anyone not until you get your Grant we do this to make sure real winners get their money. We had situations where other people claim what is not theirs and when you are making your payment do not disclose this to anyone because if you do the IRS will be inform about your Grant and the IRS will charge you 40% out of your Grant Money I hope you understand this?

Here is the information the UPS is going to ask you when they come to make your deliver your winning money to you .. UPS LOGISTICA

UPS: MSM Ltd Rep.

Ref No: XXX

Batch No: 281020001PRD

Hello, I got bad news from the UPS just now that IRS stopped them on there way coming to make your delivery this morning....IRS told the UPS that there is a Tax they must pay on the winning money before it can be deliver for you and the amount is $6000. That is the only delay we have right now and you need to make another payment of $6000 to the UPS cashier so that they can clear the tax fees and deliver your winning money to you. Get back to me asap with the MTCN Control number as soon as you make your payment. Thanks.

There are a lot of persons and sites on the Internet, offering lottery, fare well gifts and Bitcoin. The client is promised a high profit with just little investment or a gift. This is all fraud! After payment the money is gone, no profit, no gift, just loss!

Some examples, like these pages look like:

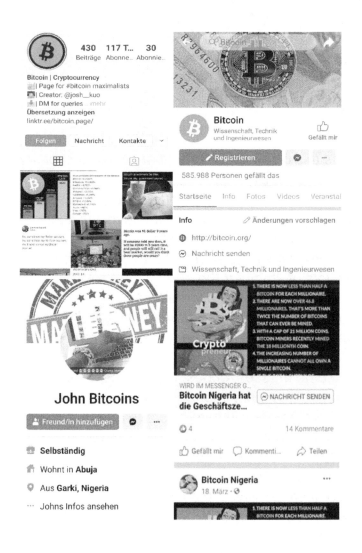

4.9. Charity or Orphanage Scam

With the charity scam, scammers try to collect money on Internet sites for welfare. This can be poor children, old people, to save animals etc. When in Australia there was a huge forest fire, a fake site on Instagram tried to collect money *to save the burned koala bears.*

The orphanage scam instead *works* with orphans.

There's this orphanage home that I used to sponsor somewhere outside ....It's about a year now that I haven't donated anything or offered any funds to them due to my work. You know it involves a lot of traveling....I just had an email from them that they need some items like shirts, shorts, shoes and whole lots of stuffs for the kids....You know I never had a child and I love children that's why am doing all this for them...With my situation now, I am in Dubai now and can't send anything out from here...am a total stranger out here..lol. I want to order some dresses, shoes, caps, verses etc to your address so that later on, I will contact the UPS Shipping Company in Iowa to come and pick it up and then send it to its destination....I would have used any of my friends address but the problem is that, this UPS Shipping Company are not in some parts of their locality....And I've also heard that there is one is Iowa which is the best, so that's why am counting on you to agree so that I can make these orphanage home know that am thinking about them as well....And you must note one thing that this doesn't involve any payment of money.. you'll be given a cheque later after the pickup.. that's within some weeks...a week or two. It's so simple, if it arrives in your address, UPS comes to pick it up and then its sent to its destination....That's all. Let's help to support these kids....I'll look forward to your address and God will richly bless both of us for raising support to these kids...Thanks

4.10. Celebrity Scam

The scammer creates a fake account on a site with the pictures and videos of a famous person. Popular are actors, pop stars but also the British queen, prince and even the king of Spain. All these are fake sites with the only goal to get money out of the victim. Famous persons don't look for relationship or money on the Internet! This is all fake!

Thank you for liking my page, support you showered on me, I hope you never stop listening to my music...you look so beautiful.

I sent you a request for a purpose, I have been busy with shows and many more, traveling, thank you all for the support and love, I appreciate. I'm looking for someone I can definitely trust cause I have got some few things I need to do and take care of without my management knowing about it so I need one of my loyal fan to handle this for me.

I am not here for jokes, and secondly Facebook do not allow any other person create a duplicate of my page, it's on their violation law ok, and I promise you, if you handle this for me, you will never regret it, the reason why I need someone to do it is because the company doesn't want any media buzz of their shutdown and as you know anything concerning my name is a big media story . I have been advised by my attorney to find someone out of my circle to give this task to and compensate them for their worries...

I got in touched by the security company where I have my brief case kept for a while which contains some huge amounts of money and some valuable documents that belongs to me.

They are shutting down in couple of days and it has been giving me some problems since I have been busy with my shows and concerts, I won't have much time to take care of these responsibilities.

Mostly I do not want my management to know about this , that's why I am looking for a trust worthy person I can talk to and give this project to take care of for me and in return I will give the person 20% of the money and this is 100 % legal free. You can email me on my personal contact.

Thanks for been a real and loyal fan my dear, and your help for me on this task would mean a lot to me my dear... All I am needing you to be able to take care of the delivery fee of the briefcase from the security company to your home, mind you i want you to please be secretive concerning this to avoid impostors and if you cannot be then i cannot work with you . I also need to let you know anything you spend on this will be re-paid back to you with an 20% Interest. If this is acceptable get back to me. I'll need you to get back to me with Your Name, address, cell number

And I'll be needing you to email the security company manager Christine on XX@gmail.com, so as for her to tell you what next needed to be done. I hope to read back from you as soon as you get this done.

Hello Mrs., how are you doing today, my name is X. I am sure Mr. X must have told you about me and who I am. Not to prolong matter, I will need you to make the payment of $300 for the shipment of the box right away, and I will need you to forward to me your full name, home address, and your phone number...

Here my personal assistant details you are to send the money to via Western Union or Walmart Money transfer ...And do get back to me with the pickup reference numbers or scan and attach the receipt to me...

How are you doing today, fine I hope. My personal assistant got the money picked up yesterday, and I am sorry I could not get back to you yesterday, I had some other situations to attend to, And I needed to hear from Mr. Tyler before I could proceed, due to you act. But I think it's alright now, because I got a message from him telling me to move on with you, that you are just trying to be careful.

Well. I would like you to know that I got Mr. X brief case off the safe it was locked, and I found out that we will have to do some change of ownership before we would be able to ship the brief case to you as it contains everything about Mr. Tyler. And has he has said that he wants this to be a secret, we will be needing to change his whole details to yours, so as to avoid the media buzz and for no one to know who actually it belongs to. So, I will be needing you to make the payment of $600, so that I can get the brief case shipped out as soon as possible.

How are you doing today, fine I hope. I got the money picked up yesterday, and I am sorry I could not get back to you yesterday, I had some other situations to attend to. Well. I would like you know that I got Mr Tracy Lawrence briefcase off the safe it was locked, and I found out that we will have to do some change of ownership before we would be able to ship the brief case to you as it contains everything about Mr Tracy Lawrence And has he has said that he wants this to be a secret, we will be needing to change his whole details to yours, so as *to avoid the media buzz and for no one to know who actually it belongs to so i will be needing you to make the payment of $600 for this to be done, so that I can get the brief case shipped out as soon as possible. We are sorry for any inconvenience this might cause you..*

4.11. Gold Scam

The fraud tries to convince the client to invest in gold or to buy gold. Instead of receiving the gold, the whole money will disappear in the darkness of Internet.

I wish you the best of this season, and abundant mercies of the Lord, I with all humility and respect. though you do not know who I am, I am the daughter of the late president of Guinea-Bissau. My father name is Joao Bernardo Vieira. He has several local mining companies in republic of Guinea and in Ghana where we mine Gold and

Diamond. My late father deposited 250kg of Gold and a lot of quantity of pure Diamond in a security company in Accra Ghana a year ago before he passed away.

I hereby informed you/your organization a full corporate offer for the sale 250 KG of 22 Karat gold dust. I urgently seek for urgent marketing/buyers and joint partnership business and I am ready to reduce my price from the International price. Base in the degree of sincerity and trust found in you. If I receive your reply. I will feed you with the relevant information in this gold business (Karat gold dust) following quantities/quality:

1. Product: AU Metal Stones of Guinea-Bissau pure Diamonds

2. Origin: Republic of Guinea-Bissau

3. Type: Alluvial Gold dust 22 Karat

4. Purity: 95%

May you give me your prompt response as to the above quotation for the business, and also the quantity of the gold dust you will buy. I really need a buyer who can come here and help me clear these goods and I am willingly to sell for them. I am looking forward to hear from you soonest.

Hello Darling, how was your day? I guess it is not as good it would be when we are together. I always do miss you a lot and wish we are together. I really wish you are here or I am there. I think of you every minute of the day and so proud to have such a precious and kind hearted woman like you in my life. You are just a dream come true, a special and a one in a million woman. I never thought that I could find someone with both outside and inner beauty like you. I feel so blessed and lucky to have found you.

I was at the meeting with the Authorities of the mining company concerning my purchase of the gold. Guess what honey? They showed me pure and quality gold in large quantities to the lightness of my heart.. The price of the gold was reduce to 29,000 USD, but I negotiated with them, including the lawyer.. We negotiated for a long time until they came to a conclusion that it will be reduce to 25,000 USD. It wasn't easy for them to accept the current price of the gold.

But there is a problem, the problem is that I always travel with cheque for my business as I have told which is the best option since it's not good to travel with a lot of cash and I hope you will agree with me on that but in this situation that I find myself now, I need some cash to make my dreams come true for this purchase. Darling, the purchase which I'm supposed to make is worth 1.8 million but I only have my cheque to pay off this and this seems to take quite some time before a cheque gets cleared honey. I do not know what to do now because they are demanding for at least a deposit of 80,000 USD, before they can reserve the gem stones for me and wait until my cheque gets cleared which may take some few more days as i was told by the bank, due to the amount.

Darling, my worry is that there is another customer and other agencies who are so waiting to purchase if I don't take immediate action. Honey, I don't want to lose this great opportunity as you know how important this business is for me and for us. I thought and thought all day but don't know what to do as i have no option left with than to share with you, my love. Please try your best to help me work this out, sweetheart. I promise, I will do an immediate wire transfer back to you once the check gets cleared. Honey, you are my only hope now and you know there is nobody else I can run through in this critical condition now. Please give me a shoulder to lean on. Let my dreams come through and let my long journey down here not be in vain.

I am so grateful to have such a special and caring woman like you in my life now. I love you because you make me look forward to each day. You are my everything, a dream come true. There are no words to express what I feel for you. There are no songs as beautiful as the music that fills my soul when I hear your voice. There are no roses as lovely as your smile. Nothing moves me like you do. There are no days brighter than the days I spend talking to you on the phone. You are my light in the darkness. There could never be words strong enough to

*express my love for you. I love you with my body,
soul, and mind. You are my everything. I love you
so much and will always do!!! I will be looking
forward to hearing from you soon & Please try your
very best to support.*

4.12. Diplomat Scam

This form of scam is used or to get money to pay for
a package to be transferred, for lost documents or
other fake stories regarding a traveller. A diplomat
will contact the victim and ask for the transfer of the
money.

*I have finally booked the flight to Ghana which is in
west Africa. It is 4 hours 50 mins flight. Somehow
long but okay. I got this flight. Take off is in 3 hours.
It's now 05:27 PM. So, the flight will take off at
08:27 PM and will probably be in Ghana 4 hours
later. I will also keep you update when I get to
Ghana. Again, thanks for your maximum
corporation. So babe, about the delaying the
diploma has been busy to some issues, so he is
very hot so he want his assistant to get on with the
package, babe and his secretary's name is,
XXX@hotmail.com so from now on you will only
have to pay accordingly to Mr. X, to make the
package successful, babe hope you understand,
now have a nice day....*

Hello Mrs. X, I will like to inform you that, the date of the ticket on the package has expired. It came to my attention that you need to make a payment of three thousand five hundred Euros (3.500), through MoneyGram money transfer to the name X.

To enable me renew the date on the package at the office over here. Before it can be allowed to join the available cargo plane in Ghana to Netherlands. Am waiting for your reply with your payment information immediately, so that the transaction will be done as fast as possible, before I lose the available flight. If the package stays long in their custody, the charges will increase. Reply me as soon as possible.

Receiver's name:

Amount to be send: 3.500 €

Receiving Destination: Ghana

Sincerely, Diplomat X

4.13 New formats for scam

Recently these new formats for romance scam appeared. Scammers adapt to time and always update their formats. Therefor the formats presented in this book are not complete! Be aware that every day scammers only work on new tricks to scam their victims!

harmful that they are considered to be
defamatory **per se** which makes a case for
a suit unless they can proof the accusations
they made .
18 U.S. Code §1038 makes that statement
constitute to a violation of chapter 2, 10,
11B, 39, 40, 44, 111, or 113B of this title .
I deal with international cases too but I will
make a lawyer in Kentucky file this at the
Southern district court of Indiana and 7th
Circuit Court of Appeals in Indiana and this
will go and on .

Prelude : J̶̶̶̶̶̶̶̶̶̶̶̶̶̶̶̶̶̶C is a rookie
company that I handle legal issues
concerning their partners . There's not and
has never been any fraudulent activity
involved with this account .
The owner has volunteered to include his
name in this procedural suit if you give
the formal consent . The bank
could've repudiated this transfer without
defaming our image and the amazing
relationship we built this limited period .

I'm no leccator but a man of integrity and I
can't be affiliated with issues of any
dubious act .

I hope to hear from you my friend .
Have a great evening

ou can say one of this tips to him to hold
m on till you make him fall and bill him
ith the billing way
you live alone ....
Honey I'm trying to organize myself
nd finish some clients requests and
ders then we can plan and meet
fterwards , the virus has set me back .
Honey sounds great let's just get to
now each other a little better then we
an plan and meet the following week
urely . I'm so eager to see you too
you live with Mom/Aunt
Honey sounds great I'm trying to
ganize some few stuffs for mom then I
an plan and come to you including
tting her CSA private nurse to come
ke care of her let's relax , I should
ganize all in a week ,
Sounds nice honey let me just prepare
me good groceries and refill moms
edication then we can plan and I will
me to you , I'm so eager to see you too

How to receive your first billing confirmation with the new format

Receiving money through the new format
is as simple as ABCD
Just say the private nurse wants her
payment this way (PayPal , wire , deposit ,
a check in her name , money order)
Just make sure it's a whites name
osimple .
Also because she will receive her payment
before she starts or resume work ..

If he accepts to pay the first CSA private
nurse billing , note this

Your first confirmation is everything , don't
involve any **Ghana** or Africa names and
fuck it up .
Receive through your old pal or someone
with a white pickup or names that's
foreign
This job is too difficult for a Ghanaian
name to fuck it up
Please be sharp on that end

90

foreign
▶ **This job is too difficult for a Ghanaian name to fuck it up**
Please be sharp on that end
Even ur PayPal email should not have a Ghana name .

✕✕✕✕

First confirmation clicks , you are headed to something great don't fuck it up , don't be greedy find a good pickup name and don't think about percentage !!
Just confirm him rightly ✅

That means he doesn't need to send money to the name you chat him with , just to the private nurse directly .

So just get him a female or white name and if he complains you say it's the private nurse information or contacts because you want it to get to her directly so she resumes work and you can come to him

ALL THE BEST !!!

Law codes

✅ *per curiam* ——of an opinion or decision) by the court as a whole rather than in the name of a particular judge

✅ **declaratory** ——- serving to declare or make known or explain
Examples - I consider the bill before us merely in the light of a declaratory law.
2️⃣ Petitioners sought declaratory relief against the enforcement of the rule

✅ **Injunctive /injunction** ——— command / order / the act of enjoining- direct order to do something /mandate

✅ **insofar** ——— to such an extent / because / taking into an account
Examples —— Insofar as I myself am concerned, I am wholly disinterested.
2️⃣ Petitioners sought an order against enforcement of the rule insofar as it prevented them from transporting firearms .

91

The only disease you should use for the new format

The whites are all familiar with it

🍂 Parkinson Disease

Summary of it
Causes are unknown but it affects people older than 60, Symptoms include Shaking, rigidity, slowness of movement, difficulty walking ,

Causes in case asked :::: Doctor said Old age and genetics maybe

Treatment is by Supportive Care / Medications , meaning she's need a CSA private nurse .

The person can't do nothing
They just relax at home and get someone to take care of them .

So during billing you just get a private nurse she charges you bill him and pay and go to him ..
On GOD

DEMENTIA DISEASE

It's a disease caused by the gradual decrease in the ability to think and remember that is severe to affect daily function
Causes in case asked :::: Doctor said Old age and genetics

Symptoms include

Decreased ability to think and remember, emotional problems, problems with language, decreased motivation

Treatments::: Supportive Care / Medications
Meaning your mom is almost mad but not really mad , forgets easily and can't do nothing

So she needs a private nurse or she's been using a private care for a while now

Simple On GOD

92

Azheirmer Disease

is a chronic neurodegenerative disease
that usually starts slowly and gradually
worsens over time

Chronic means constant or having long
duration .

Symptoms include Difficulty in
remembering recent events, problems
with language, disorientation, mood
swings

Causes if asked ::: Genetics or Head Injury
It's pretty worse form of Dementia

Treatment :: Medication / Supportive care

All the best !!
How to receive money with the new format

Receiving money through the new format
is as simple as ABCD
Just say the private nurse wants her
payment this way (PayPal , wire , deposit ,
a check in her name , money order)
Just make sure it's a female name simple .
Also because she will receive her payment
before she starts or resume work ..

That means he doesn't need to send
money to the name you chat him with ,
just to the private nurse directly .

So just get him a female name and if he
complains you say it's the private nurse
information because you want it to get to
her directly so she resumes work and you
can come to him

ALL THE BEST !!!

93

5. Where and how Scammers act

Scammers are on all Internet platforms and dating sites. Facebook, Instagram, Twitter but also on paid sites like Parship and others. They even prefer the paid sites because a client, who can pay the membership on such a dating portal, is for sure rich, they believe. The scammer takes a long-term membership there because this is cheaper. To prove his identity, a picture is loaded on the computer and confirms the identity via the mobile phone or a fake identity card is presented to the platform and the scammer easily gets access to the paid site.

Here the exchange of information in a scammer

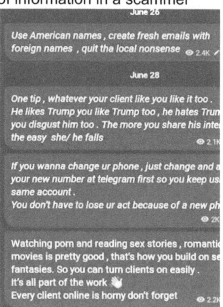

group on *Telegram*:

The following lists show the most common internet sites, where scammers work, though the professional ones work also on paid dating sites.

AmericanSingles.com
Amor
Asia FriendFinder
Asian Singles Connect
BBW Personals Plus
BigChurch.com
BlackSingles.com
Canadian Personals
Catholic Mingle
Chemistry
ChristianCafe.com
ChristianMingle.com
Date.ca
Date.com
DatingDirect
eHarmony
FriendFinder
Friends Reunited Dating
Gay.com
Indian FriendFinder
InterracialMatch.com
It's Just Lunch
JDate
Jewish FriendFinder
Lavalife
Lavalife PRIME
Match.com
Match.com UK
Matchmaker.com
Mate1
MillionaireMatch.com
MillionaireMate.com
Muslima.com
OutPersonals.com
Passion.com
PerfectMatch.com
PositiveSingles.com
Prime Singles
RSVP
Senior FriendFinder
SeniorMatch.com
Shaadi Matrimonial

Single Christian Net
Single Parents Mingle
SinglesNet.com
Sugardaddie.com
UK Singles Connect
€WealthyMen.com
Yahoo! Personals
Award Winning Dating
ChristianCafe.com
eHarmony
Lavalife
Lavalife PRIME
Match.com
MillionaireMatch.com
Passion.com
Senior FriendFinder
Yahoo! Personals
Religious Dating
BigChurch.com
Catholic Mingle
ChristianCafe.com
ChristianMingle.com
eHarmony
JDate
Jewish FriendFinder
Single Christian Net
Dating Over 50
Lavalife PRIME
PerfectMatch.com
Prime Singles
Senior FriendFinder
SeniorMatch.com
Ethnic Dating
Amor
Asia FriendFinder
Asian Singles Connect
BlackSingles.com
Indian FriendFinder
InterracialMatch.com
Muslima.com
Shaadi Matrimonial
Gay & Lesbian Personals
Gay.com
OutPersonals.com
Million Plus Members
AmericanSingles.com
Amor

Date.com
DatingDirect
eHarmony
FriendFinder
Gay.com
Lavalife
Match.com
Match.com UK
Matchmaker.com
Mate1
Passion.com
PerfectMatch.com
RSVP
Shaadi Matrimonial
SinglesNet.com
Yahoo! Personals
Miscellaneous Sites
BBW Personals Plus
PositiveSingles.com
Mobile Phone Dating
Date.com
DatingDirect
Lavalife
Match.com
RSVP
Shaadi Matrimonial
Popular Match Systems
Chemistry
eHarmony
PerfectMatch.com
Matchmaking Services
It's Just Lunch
Single Parents Dating
Single Parents Mingle
Australia Dating
RSVP
Canadian Dating
Canadian Personals
Date.ca
Date.com
Lavalife
Yahoo! Personals
UK Dating
DatingDirect
Friends Reunited Dating
Match.com UK
UK Singles Connect

Sexy Singles
Gay.com
Lavalife
Passion.com
Wealthy Singles Dating
MillionaireMatch.com
MillionaireMate.com
Sugardaddie.com
WealthyMen.com
Free Dating Sites
Down To Earth
OkCupid
PlentyOfFish.com
Dating Profile Help
E-Cyrano
Look Better Online
AsianPeopleMeet.com
BabyBoomerPeopleMeet.com
BBPeopleMeet.com
BlackBabyBoomerMeet.com
BlackChristianPeoplemeet.com
BlackPeopleMeet.com
CatholicPeopleMeet.com
ChinesePeopleMeet.com
DemocraticPeopleMeet.com
DivorcedPeopleMeet.com
IndiaMatch.com
InterracialPeopleMeet.com
JPeopleMeet.com
LatinoPeopleMeet.com
LDSPlanet.com
LittlePeopleMeet.com
LoveAndSeek.com
MarriagemindedPeopleMeet.com
PetPeopleMeet.com
RepublicanPeopleMeet.com
SeniorBlackPeoplemeet.com
SeniorPeopleMeet.com
SingleParentMeet.com
SPARKSNETWORK SITES
AmericanSingles.com
AdventistSinglesConnection.com
AsianSinglesConnection.com
BlackChristianSingles.com
BlackSingles.com
CanadianPersonals.net
CatholicMingle.com

98

ChristianMingle.com
CollegeLuv.com
Cupid.co.il
Date.ca
Date.co.uk
DeafSinglesConnection.com
Facelink.com
GreekSinglesConnection.com
HurryDate.com
IndianMatrimonialNetwork.com
InterracialSingles.net
ItalianSinglesConnection.com
JDate.co.il
JDate.co.uk
JDate.com
JewishMingle.com
Kizmeet
LatinSinglesConnection.com
LDSMingle.com
LDSSingles.com
MilitarySinglesConnection.com
Moretolove.com
PrimeSingles.net
SingleParentsMingle.com
UKSinglesConnection.com

Some scammers prefer lesbian and gay sites because they say that these people are *easy* to scam and will pay for sure. Some male scammers prefer men, because *it is easier to scam a man with fake sex video calls.*

"The scammer always controls the victim, but the victim never controls the scammer!"

The typical questions and answers a fraud will ask a client to get control over him or her are like the

99

following. With the time the scammer knows all details about the victim, tries to isolate the person from family and friends and takes over control, brainwashing and manipulating the client by contacting him or her all the time pretending to be madly in love. The scammer will do and say everything to make the client happy. Then something *happens* and the scammer needs *help.* If the scammer does not get what he wants, he disappears.

Where are you from...?

On my father's side it is U.S.A and Germany and on my mother's side it is Ghana

Do you like Jazz?

Do you have any fun?

I love to cook, garden, traveling, go to movies, read, computer, dine out, walk around town, go hiking, camping, or just sit and relax at home...

Are you single, married or divorced...?

Do you have any children? If Yes How many children do you have...?

I'm single and never been married.

What are you looking for in a relationship and what do you dislike in a woman....?

I'm Looking for good and kind man, loyal, caring, thoughtful, creative, compassionate, imaginative, serious, sensual and passionate......But dislike men who lie, cheat, dishonest, disrespectful, and who just play tricks, and game on their women...

Can you please tell me more about yourself...?

I'm 5'9 tall, and am 29 years old, I have Salt and pepper Hair, blue eyes, and I'm honest, family oriented, love to please the chosen men, respectful, honest, reliable, cheerful, sensitive and loyal...

Where were you born and raised up ....?

Can we share photos...

How big is your family and are your parent there...?

How many times have you been married...?

Are pets an important part of your life?

What's your religion...?

Do you smoke cigarettes or drink alcohol or take drugs...?

How many years have you lived alone...?

Do you enjoy being alone?

Are you a passionate person...?

When did you last have sex..?

Are you into a serious relationship with someone?

Well, if you have not been taken by someone special can we be serious with each other by fixing time to meet every day on here to chat and get to know each other very much as well, from there we will see how God will lead as to...

What is your favourite colour ...?

What's your favourite foods & drinks...?

What are you mostly afraid of in a relationship...?

Oh Yes, I know it's hard to trust but I don't give up in trusting the right woman who I love to spend the rest of my lifetime with....

How romantic are you...?

What are your favourite sports or game do you like to play...?

How do you feel about relocating for a relationship...?

What types of music or movies or TV Shows you like...?

Do you have any tattoos or body piercing...?

What's your star sign...?

When in a relationship, how much personal space do you generally find you need...?

How often do you lose your temper...? Practically never...

If your life partner had a bad day, what is the first thing you would do for her...?

How many female/male friends have you had before...?

I have many male and female friends but I chose few as my best friend because some friends are very dangerous. they can give you bad advice. ......Also, some can tell you something which you don't like and that's going to tear up your relationship …

What have you learned about yourself from every past relationship...?

Have you been hurt before...?

I truly believe that God Himself brought you down from the glorious heavens above to be forever my angel and show you how very big my love is for you – every day, every night, every time, all my life. I love you, I will hold you all my life.

You know it's true love when the butterflies in your stomach make you feel like you can fly away, and true Love is never artificial; it's always pure.

Honey, I will never use force on you not even by words. In your presence, I will always be honest, transparent and sincere. I want always to be at your side.

I will love you with every beat of my heart! You are the love of my life and I am glad that I picked you to fall in love with.

Some are pretty, some are cute, some have the eyes, some have the looks. Beauty is something that cannot be defined, but if it could be defined, in you it would be confined.

The best day in my life was the day I married you

The best thing in my life is you

I cannot imagine a single day without you

I've said it once, and I'll say it again

I love you!!

I think that the Gods must have been asleep the day you were born. Only then would they have let such a beautiful angel escape to earth! I love you.

My love for you is deeper than the deepest ocean

Taller than the tallest mountain

Hotter than the hottest desert

And denser than the densest of forests

My love for you is truly eternal

I love you

I want to love you more than forever because even eternity is not enough time for me to express my love for you.

I am afraid of death not because I fear death itself. I am afraid of death because I know that even the heavens cannot be as beautiful as you. I love you my dear wife!

I believe in God, I believe in miracles and I believe in angels, because it is a miracle that the Gods sent an angel like you in my life. Love you darling.

I have stopped making wishes on spotting falling stars. Do you know why? Because I have you and that's all I want in my life.

I want you to know that I am yours today, tomorrow and forever. I never knew what true love was until I met you. I love you dear.

Some scammers don't know what to do with certain questions of the client. They are overextended and have to ask their *boss,* what they should answer:

Boss, what about words with emojis like this?
6:20 PM

One or two emojis is coherent , anything than that is like teenager typing .
7:27 PM 19:27

Those times for yahoo ,msn wey we dey paste 🖌️/🤍 like a painter , that life ended in 2007 abeg you ..

Let's mature , Scam red flags ▶

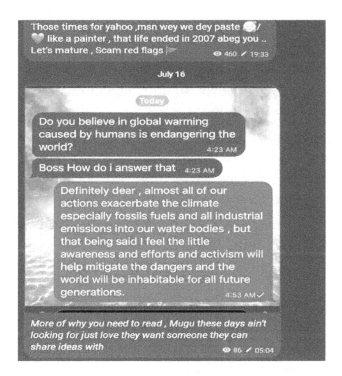

6. Fake Calls

Few frauds do call to prove to the victim that they
are real. Sometimes the client will receive an audio
call with just the fake picture appearing on the
phone. Scammers use phone numbers from all over
the world: USA, UK, Germany etc. The accent and
the way of expression of African people is
completely different from American or UK persons.
To explain that, the scammer pretends that one of
his parents is from a different country or he didn't
grow up in the US. The scammers use different

107

expressions, for example *"I want to take my bath"* instead of *"I want to take my shower"*. But there are also devices, that change the voice and even the accent. You can be never sure to speak to a real American or UK person!

Others do fake video calls. They use special devices to manipulate WhatsApp and play a mute video in. In most of the cases, they don't talk. A video is played for around 5 minutes. Then the scammer pretends that the network is bad and goes offline and says that he will call later. Others manipulate the video and really speak. So, the client will see the fake video with the scammer speaking for some minutes.

A fake video call can be identified by the following signs: The video is flickering, is not clear, no one is speaking, the call is for just some minutes, if someone is speaking the lips and the words are not mutual (excuse: *the network is bad here*). To find the prove, the called person can ask the caller to make a certain movement with the hand, to go to another room, to speak, to make a certain sign etc. The scammer cannot do that because he is playing a prepared video on the phone or computer. To make a fake video call, the scammer has to change his VPN and turn the fake identity on. These fake VPNS can be easily gotten on the Internet.

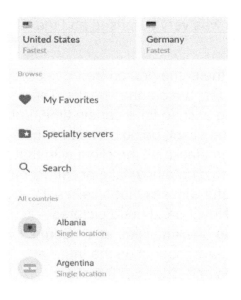

One day a scammer was faking an American guy, pretending he is a lady. The American guy called the fraud unexpectedly and that one forgot to switch on the fake identity. He picked up the video call from the American and that one saw, that the *beautiful lady* he was speaking to for a month and to whom he had already sent money, was a young black man from Ghana. The situation escalated and the black man was blocked by the American.

A Nigerian guy tried to scam a white woman. The white woman called him on video, speaking perfectly Nigerian language and telling him to *fuck off*. After being the victim of a scam, the white lady had learned the Nigerian language to follow up on scammers! The guy was very surprised and the scam was over.

Sex video calls use the same procedure. A video is played with sex scenes, but no one speaks. The client is just watching a video for a certain time, but the scammer sees the client, doing certain things. Some record that and blackmail the client with that video after or use it to create new fake accounts on the Internet. Be careful with sex video calls – it could be recorded! Never send nude pictures – it could be also used to blackmail you after! Some frauds create new fake accounts on the Internet with the new pictures and videos of the client.

In most cases though the scammers try to avoid phone and video calls. They only do it if they must, to prove that they are *real*. Otherwise they tell the client the following:

Am using a prepaid phone.... I can't receive or make calls it's a contract phone and right now am living on a low income I can't afford to pay my phone bills. I only have unlimited text on it if you don't mind, we can only exchange text okay.

7. Behind the Scam Scenes
Some scammers live together in *scammer houses* with a chairman leading and controlling them. The colleagues are called *brothers.* They *share work* and sometimes a victim *speaks* with different

frauds. They don't have any respect, the Maga or Mugu (the victim) is passed on to the colleague for chat if the scammer is busy with the words *"take her!"*. The victim has no personal value for the scammer. For him she or he is just like a *cash machine*. If a scammer did not succeed to get money, he will mostly come back with another fake profile to the same victim to try it again. Sometimes he passes on the victim to his colleague, who then tries to *find his luck*.

There are lists with detailed information about the clients: income, kids, divorced or not, car, house etc. The scammers have access to these lists and some know already details about the future client, when they contact him or her.

In public some scammers show that they are *business men*, well dressed, with big cars, women and cash in their pockets. Nothing is too expensive for them. They show what they have. Behind the scenes though, there is a lot of *competition*, *envy* and even *homicide* if one scammer gets money, but the other one not. The background of the frauds is not *like in heaven*.

If they are sceptical about the identity of a client, they *greet* with *alaye*. That means something like *are you a scammer as well* to avoid time wasters.

Usually they are young, between 20 and 35 years, they claim not to be married or to be widowed (very often) but in reality, some of them are married with children and they do the scam to feed their family.

If the client finds out that something is wrong and tells it to the fraud the answer will be: *"You don't trust me, you hurt me with that, I never said that, It's just a misunderstanding, I love you so much, Please forgive me, You understood that wrong, I didn't mean that, etc."* In the end the fault is given to the victim: *"It's all your fault"*. Scammers have psychological knowledge and they follow a plan, the *format*, they have chosen for the respective client. They do everything to make the client happy, they adapt their points of view to those of the victim in order to get closer to him or her. Pretending to be jealous, the scammer starts to take over control, not leaving time for the victim to get a clear mind and recognise certain things. *"That nonsense I will knock you out!"*

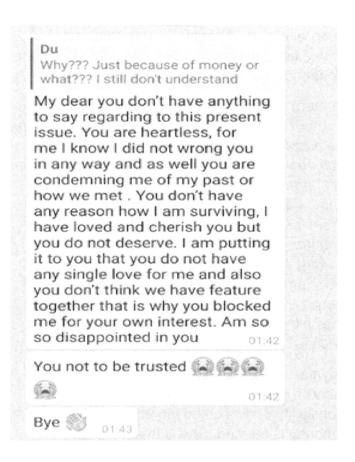

Du
Why??? Just because of money or what??? I still don't understand

My dear you don't have anything to say regarding to this present issue. You are heartless, for me I know I did not wrong you in any way and as well you are condemning me of my past or how we met . You don't have any reason how I am surviving, I have loved and cherish you but you do not deserve. I am putting it to you that you do not have any single love for me and also you don't think we have feature together that is why you blocked me for your own interest. Am so so disappointed in you   01:42

You not to be trusted 😭 😭 😭
😭   01:42

Bye 👋   01:43

Usually the victim is blocked on the account of the Internet platform, where he or she was *found,* after a short time with the excuse that the account was hacked and is no more there. This has the purpose to avoid the victim to see how many new requests and followers the scammer has there. Scammers have a lot of different Internet accounts and sites. They are always online to find new clients and chatting with a lot of people (men and women) at the same time, minimum 5 because maybe 3 of the 5 will not pay.

Scammers use a lot of excuses when they are busy with other *clients* and don't have time to chat. *"I am at the hospital now, I am at the gym now, I am at church now, I am at a child's birthday party, The line is bad here, I have no Internet connection, I am driving, I have a headache, I am at a funeral, My brother was arrested and I had to get him out, My neighbours are here, I am sorry I slept off yesterday, I was doing cleaning and washing etc."* Some scammers throw the client out of the phone line when they receive another, more important, phone call, showing that they have no respect for the victim.

Mostly the woman receives a marriage proposal online with the purpose that now she is in the responsibility when something unexpected happens and money is needed. She is the *future wife.* Romantic moments must be *worked out,* before they can happen. Sometimes fake sex video calls are done. The scammer records the woman and blackmails her after with the video. Also, nude pictures are requested „*It's just between me and you*", in reality everything is used against the woman or men to get money. Also new fake profiles are established with the *material* gained and new persons are scammed with the woman's or man's profile.

Some scammers admit that they are not the real person on the fake picture, they send their real picture, do video calls and audio calls. One thing remains, they still expect one day to get money from the white person. They sometimes are very depressive and down, even crying. Why? Someone has blocked them without paying the expected money or some of the Internet fake accounts have been deleted, that *hurts*! Then they pretend that they will change, that everything they did was bad, that from now on they will be decent and look for a work. *"I can't lie to you, then I would lie to myself. Can we build up a future together? When I come to your country, will I get a good job there? I want to create a family with you. I want a baby with you. Will you allow me to have the baby with someone else, I just make her pregnant but I will always be your husband. Will you send me invitation? You can come also to Nigeria."*

OK thank you

Where are you from

I'm from Nigeria but live in
Ghana

Most of the scammers use drugs like weed or
Codeine, calling on video showing it, or they are so
high, that they cannot think or speak in a clear way.

They pretend that they have promised to *grandma*
to marry soon, so she can *die in peace.* They show
sisters, brothers and other family members on video
to gain the confidence of the client.

After having showed their real identity to the victim,
some pretend to have stopped the scam because
they are deeply in love with her or him. But now
they need money to pay daily living costs,
sometimes medical treatment or clothes etc. The
scam goes on. Usually a scammer spends the
whole day in bed, in underwear because in Africa it

is hot, speaking to a lot of clients and smoking a lot of weed or taking other drugs. They have changing moods, one day they are very happy, the next day completely down, nearly depressive. Sometimes they are also aggressive: *"I shoot you if you speak to someone else!"*. Sometimes they are loving and caring, the next day cold and distant. They have changing opinions, moods, likes and dislikes, depending on with whom they speak. Sometimes their energy is so different that one thinks that he or she speaks to a different person. They are like *chameleons*, always adapting to the respective client.

Really 21:14 ✓✓

Yah 21:15

You did not tell me that 21:15 ✓✓

But I told you I will stop the internet stuff which I promise you that I will stop 21:16

I have done dat 21:16

OK I am glad to hear that 21:16 ✓✓

And what could you do instead 21:17 ✓✓

Am home thinking all day 21:17

I understand 21:17 ✓✓

Even asking my friends who are working with the government to get a space for me to work 21:18

Oh that sounds great, am happy about that 21:18 ✓✓

I was worried about you 21:19 ✓✓

Sometimes am tired of sitting at home doing nothing 21:20

Yes I imagine that 21:20 ✓✓

Use your intelligence to create something 21:20 ✓✓

Is really boring 21:20

You are very smart 21:20 ✓✓

Yes honey there are lots of business to do , but I don't have the money to set it up 21:21

Is somehow any way 21:22

You will find a way, am sure 21:22 ✓✓

Yah 21:24

Thinking of it 21:24

Sure I will 21:24

118

The fraud tries to manipulate the victim by telling *"but you really should start a work now for our future, do some jogging because you are getting fat"*. They never keep their promises because in the next minute they forgot, what they have promised. They forget dates, facts, projects, things etc. They cannot keep in mind everything because they are speaking to many people. If the victim tells them about a problem he or she has, the scammer disappears quickly because he is not interested in that. If the victim blocks the scammer, it might happen that he follows up on her or him, calling 20 times a day on phone, creating a new Internet account and begging like a dog to take him back. The fault for everything is given to the victim: *"It is all your fault, you are crazy. Always remember that in Nigeria there is someone who really loves you."* The scam continues. The love songs sent by the client are often passed on to other clients to make them fall for the scammer.

A scammer has busy times during the year: Christmas, Valentine's day, Easter, end of June when in Europe people receive the holiday allowance. *"I really need your gifts here, I am getting old, I need someone to take care for, I want to live in Canada, what will you do to make me happy (everything from the heart is welcome)? etc."*

The character of the scammers is split. Or they are cold and brutal or they are servile and begging. They pretend to be jealous on the victim. *"I kill you if you speak to someone else".* Mostly they are unhappy persons, they have no feelings, they are only happy if they receive money. That money though will not stay with them for a long time. Some spend it quickly on a party, others buy cars or motorbikes. One guy bought a motorbike with the stolen money from a woman and died in a bike accident. The church and God are very important for them. Some ask the victim to read psalms and visit church.

There are scammers who never give up. Even after months, they still try to get in contact with the victim again. They call with different numbers or create new accounts on the Internet and write message requests, pretending that *they are still in love and that they have never forgotten their only great love.*

8. Ten Golden Rules

1) Be aware that **most** people on the Internet sites, also the paid ones, **are fakes!** If you open your account to a scammer, he will usually also try to contact your friends and add them.

2) **No beautiful man or woman** looks on the Internet for a soul mate!

3) Scammers mostly use **hearts, teddy bears, children, flowers and animals** on their sites! Check also the **friends list.** Are there many black, Arabic or other foreign people, strange pictures etc.

An example of a fake profile with the stolen pictures of the model Brian Haugen on Instagram.

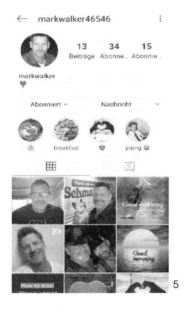

5

4) A real person **will not write you** after sending you a friend request, and if yes, just a greeting. The scammer will **overflow you with compliments**, trying to put you on **WhatsApp or Hangouts**.

5) The scammer **quickly falls in love** with you. Some don't even need one day for it. Typical scammer expressions are: My queen, my king, honey, my love, sweetie, baby, sweetheart, my darling etc.

---

[5] https://www.brianhaugen.net/

6) At the beginning the scammer **will ask you a lot of questions** to get information. Then he starts the respective format of scam.

7) **Never send money** to someone you have not seen in person!!! Scammers are very clever; they manipulate their victims and don't hesitate to make the victim feel guilty for not sending the money to them. Always demand the scammer to meet personally! Video call the new contact. If the phone is not picked up, something is wrong!

8) There are many **groups** on the Internet, where you can find help. Contact them and ask for help to find out, if the person you are speaking to **is real or not**. There are also **sites where fake pictures** are exposed. With **Google picture search** you can search by yourself on the Internet. Just copy the picture of the profile in and search. You will find the real person.

9) Again: **never send money!!!** But if you have, go to the next police station and report it. Keep evidence of the chats, pictures and documents you have received from the scammer.

10) Love yourself more!!! A scammer is **not worth being regretted** after having you left. Usually he will not remember you after 3 days and has forgotten your name, because he has passed on to the next victim!

9. Where Victims can find Additional Help

Victims can find help on scammer fighter groups like

https://www.scamwatch.gov.au/types-of-scams/dating-romance

https://www.consumer.ftc.gov/articles/what-you-need-know-about-romance-scams

https://www.polizei-beratung.de/themen-und-tipps/betrug/scamming/

https://www.ag.state.mn.us/Consumer/Publications/OnlineDatingRomanceScams.asp

https://www.aarp.org/money/scams-fraud/info-2020/online-romance-scams-experts.html

https://www.facebook.com/Frauds-And-Scammers-194649214387843/

https://www.facebook.com/groups/654601751605048/

or reading additional literature like

https://www.amazon.de/Fraudsters-Nigeria-Nigerian-Challenges-English-ebook/dp/B07M6M6K1Q/ref=sr_1_1?__mk_de_DE=%C3%85M%C3%85%C5%BD%C3%95%C3%91&dchild=1&keywords=young+fraudsters+in+nigeria&qid=1594482159&sr=8-1

https://www.amazon.de/My-Dear-Chibuzor-complete-English-ebook/dp/B07VVSVC2B/ref=sr_1_1?__mk_de_DE=%C3%85M%C3%85%C5%BD%C3%95%C3%91&dchild=1&keywords=my+dear+chibuzor&qid=1594482204&sr=8-1

https://www.amazon.de/Woman-Behind-Smile-Ultimate-Betrayal-ebook/dp/B01MQ2A9L8/ref=sr_1_2?__mk_de_DE=%C3%85M%C3%85%C5%BD%C3%95%C3%91&dchild=1&keywords=the+woman+behind+the+smile&qid=1594482240&sr=8-2

The best way though is not to become a victim!

Don't accept requests from strangers! Don't send money to people you have not seen personally! Be careful with personal data! Protect yourself!

Charming a scam victim (Yoruba language):

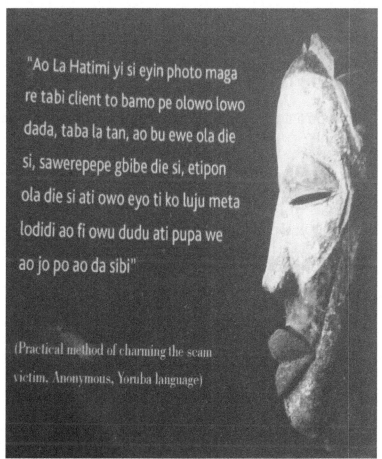

"Ao La Hatimi yi si eyin photo maga re tabi client to bamo pe olowo lowo dada, taba la tan, ao bu ewe ola die si, sawerepepe gbibe die si, etipon ola die si ati owo eyo ti ko luju meta lodidi ao fi owu dudu ati pupa we ao jo po ao da sibi"

(Practical method of charming the scam victim. Anonymous, Yoruba language)

6

---

[6] Stevenson, Tara: My dear Chibuzor book cover

Pink: Are you a heartbreaker

I keep thinkin' bout that little sparkle in your eye

Is it a light from the Angels or your Devil deep inside?

What about the way you say you love me all the time?

Are you liftin' me up to Heaven just to drop me down the line?

There's a ring around my finger

But will you change your mind?

And you tell me that I'm beautiful

But that could be a lie

Are you a heartbreaker?

Maybe you want me for the ride

What if I'm fallin' for a heartbreaker?

And everything is just a lie

I won't be livin' here alive

And I won't be livin' here alive, no

126

Temporary happiness is like waiting for the knife

'Cause I'm always watchin' for someone to show the darker side

So maybe I'll sit back and just enjoy all this for now

Watch it all play out, see if you really stick around

But there's always this one question

That keeps me up at night

Are you my greatest love

Or disappointment in my life?

Are you a heartbreaker?

Maybe you want me for the ride

What if I'm fallin' for a heartbreaker?

And everything is just a lie

I won't be livin' here alive

I might as well lay down and die

I'm holding on with both hands

And both feet, oh

Promise that you won't pull the rug

Out from under me

Are you a heartbreaker?

Maybe you want me for the ride

I pray to God you're not a heartbreaker

This time around I won't survive

'Cause if I'm fallin' for a heartbreaker

And everything is just a lie

And I won't be livin' here alive

And I might as well lay down and die, oh

I won't be livin' here alive [7]

10. Bibliography

[7] https://www.songtexte.com/songtext/pnk/heartbreaker-1b965db8.html

Uzochukwu, Mike: *Young Fraudsters In Nigeria*. United States: Amazon Self Publishing 2018.

Stevenson, Tara: *My dear Chibuzor*. Poland: Amazon Self Publishing 2019.

Internet sources :

Brian Haugan: https://www.brianhaugen.net/ (8.3.2020)

Facebook: https://www.facebook.com/ (8.3.2020)

Instagram: https://www.instagram.com/ (8.3.2020)

Jeff Sorensen: https://www.instagram.com/jeffreyyscott/?hl=de (7.7.2020)

Pink Songtext Heartbreaker: https://www.songtexte.com/songtext/pnk/heartbreaker-1b965db8.html (8.3.2020)

About the authors

Akoma Ntoso is a black - white couple, who fights against romance scam on the Internet.

After one year of research, a lot of information and background knowledge was available. To warn people all over the world, the decision was taken, to write a book about this phenomenon.